Irwin H. Polishook
Hunter College

ROGER WILLIAMS, JOHN COTTON AND RELIGIOUS FREEDOM

A Controversy in New and Old England

Prentice-Hall, Inc., Englewood Cliffs, New Jersey

AMERICAN HISTORICAL SOURCES SERIES:
Research and Interpretation

LORMAN RATNER, Editor

PRENTICE-HALL INTERNATIONAL, INC., *London*
PRENTICE-HALL OF AUSTRALIA, PTY. LTD., *Sydney*
PRENTICE-HALL OF CANADA, LTD., *Toronto*
PRENTICE-HALL OF INDIA PRIVATE LTD., *New Delhi*
PRENTICE-HALL OF JAPAN, INC., *Tokyo*

For My Wife Sheila

Current printing (last digit):
10 9 8 7 6 5 4 3 2 1

© 1967 by PRENTICE-HALL, INC.
Englewood Cliffs, New Jersey

Library of Congress Catalog Card No.: 67-20229 *1/71*

Printed in the United States of America

EDITOR'S FOREWORD

Roger Williams, John Cotton and Religious Freedom: A Controversy in New and Old England is part of the American Historical Sources Series, a series devoted to the exploration of aspects of American history and to the process of interpreting historical evidence. The introduction to each volume will be followed by some of the original documents used to prepare the essay. Readers are thus invited to share the experience of turning raw evidence into history. The essays have been written especially for this series and represent contributions to historical knowledge as well as demonstrations in the writing of history based on sources included in this work.

The controversy between the Massachusetts Bay Colony and Roger Williams, which began with Williams' banishment from Massachusetts in 1635, involved a prolonged struggle over the relationship of church and state and the nature of religious freedom. Roger Williams has been variously described as either an apostle of American democracy or a stubborn fanatic, while the Massachusetts hierarchy, represented by John Cotton, has been viewed in such opposing images as practical statesmen or reactionary persecutors. It is rare that a balanced judgment is rendered.

Professor Polishook's discussion does not prejudge the issues and events contested by Williams and Cotton. When the Puritans settled Massachusetts they had no intention of separating church and state, nor was it their desire to advocate liberty of conscience. To most Protestants of the seventeenth century the doctrines of Roger Williams meant anarchy, the collapse of social order, a final attack on the Reformation. Seen in these terms, it is easy to comprehend the willingness of John Cotton and other Massachusetts leaders to refute Roger Williams. The very fact that Williams was orthodox in his Calvinism and raised questions that were crucial to Protestants made it necessary to answer him convincingly and effectively. The exchanges between Williams and Cotton provide evidence of the vigorous arguments among Protestants regarding the correct proportions of religious liberty and order.

The story of the challenge which Roger Williams held for his contemporaries in New and Old England is developed in this study. To understand the questions and terms of the Williams-Cotton debate is to encounter one of the most difficult problems ever to face the western world.

LORMAN RATNER

CONTENTS

Roger Williams, John Cotton and Religious Freedom

The colonists of the western hemisphere were not Americans. The countless people who crossed an ocean in one of the most remarkable migrations of human history did not leave behind their former ways and aspirations. To them the newly discovered continents were merely extensions of European civilization, places in which they might fulfill destinies otherwise barred if they stayed at home. The traditions and customs they brought with them were transplanted but not necessarily transformed. In this sense, the uprooted people of seventeenth-century Europe resisted change in their new environment. The average colonist looked to a past civilization in order to reconstruct his life in the New World.

Religious freedom was not part of the colonial inheritance in America. The mass of immigrants expected uniformity of worship and demanded the persecution of notorious dissenters. Even those who fled from the Old World because of persecution had no intention of favoring religious freedom in America. Persecuted and persecutor alike agreed that liberty of worship should be forbidden.

A combination of factors, proceeding from dogma and politics, formed the colonial legacy of religious persecution. To the extent that one was sure of the word of God and with that certainty embodied in a positive, clearly developed system of doctrine, other beliefs, of necessity, were thought of as debased by varying degrees of error. Since there is but one truth, taught the European heritage, dissent is false and dangerous.

Reinforcing conviction as a source of intolerance was its identification with a visible Church. During the medieval period the Roman Catholic Church established itself as the single custodian of Christian truth. As such, it came to understand that its universal validity precluded the possibility of toleration. ᶠObviously the Church should allow no quarter to dissenters whose conflicting views disgraced God's worship and endangered the souls of innocent victims tempted by erroneous ideas.ˌ "A spark should be extinguished, fermentation removed, a putrid limb amputated, an infected animal segregated," Jerome declared, in a spirit predisposed to the persecution of religious heretics. Repellent as the doctrine of persecution may appear, it was defended by reasonable and godly men during the Middle Ages as an act of Christian charity. For example, Augustine, who was probably the most influential theorist of the period, explained that intolerance "is a righteous persecution, which the Church of Christ inflicts upon the impious." Men are persecuted, he observed, not out of malice, but "in the spirit of love," seeking to save those who stand on the brink of damnation. Such intense conviction sustained the philosophy of religious persecution.

The exaltation of faith also led to persecution by the state. To theologians it was logically absurd for the state to punish common criminals, while heretics, whose crimes were considered far more heinous, were not constrained. The ordinary murderer destroyed a person in this life only, but the heretic killed a soul forever! This analogy drew church and state together in the Middle Ages by justifying state intervention on behalf of religious uniformity. Likewise, whenever the enormity of heresy was magnified the invitation to state action was compelling. A king or civil ruler served God by restraining both religious and secular crimes, especially since the former were much more perilous.

Secular authorities needed little encouragement to extend their control over religious life. After all, the Church was a powerful institution and its strength might be harnessed to support the state. The closer the connection between the two, the more an attack on one became a blow against the other. Matters of faith, which might otherwise have been considered a private affair, were questions of public concern. Dissent became sedition. Furthermore, it was not difficult to justify the use of force against heretics on allegedly temporal grounds. Religious persecution was often considered a means of preventing the wrath of God and the punishments meted out to a blasphemous and unrighteous people. The disease of heresy was thought to be contagious and, as the Bible warned, worldly affliction was God's fury for human imperfection. Little wonder, then, that civil officers were ever watchful to blot out the first outpourings of nonconformity.

The inheritance of religious persecution was not directly challenged by the Protestant Reformation. If anything, many of the most prominent reformers were avid in denouncing the concept of religious freedom. Ironically, the increasing dissent of sixteenth-century Europe gave rise to tragic episodes of persecution. Although Protestantism emphasized the right of private judgment and the sufficiency of individual faith for salvation, neither Martin Luther nor John Calvin intended to sponsor a system which condoned liberty of conscience. For each man there was only one truth, a single Church of God, and an imperative need for perfection after the millennium of Catholic error. "Heretics are not to be disputed with, but condemned unheard," Luther cried out, "and whilst they perish by fire, the faithful ought to pursue the evil to its source, and bathe their hands in the blood of the Catholic bishops, and of the Pope, who is a devil in disguise." John Calvin's views were little different. The case of Michael Servetus, a Spanish physician and theologian who denied the divinity of Christ, showed clearly that Calvin would be ruthless in suppressing heresy. Upon Servetus' appearance in Geneva in 1553, Calvin denounced him as a notorious heretic and defended his execution as a proper vindication of the glory of God. With few exceptions, the leading Protestants shared the intolerance of the medieval past.

Despite the revolutions that were unsettling Europe on the eve of colonization, the doctrine of persecution was passed on and renewed. It arrived in America and in New England relatively undiluted. The overwhelming number of settlers in the area of Massachusetts Bay were essentially English Calvinists. Their approach to the problem of religious dissent was little different from the culture of which they had been a part.

The famous controversy with Roger Williams over religious freedom must have astounded the leaders of the Massachusetts Bay Colony. How could Williams have mistaken the purpose of the Massachusetts experiment? Was it ever intended that Massachusetts should be a land of many conflicting opinions, instead of the refuge for God's only truth? Roger Williams and his passionate plea for liberty of conscience stood in sharp contrast to the familiar and moderate understandings of the Puritan leadership. The dispute dramatically illustrated the divisive nature of Protestantism in America. Williams' attack on Massachusetts was drawn from a body of Protestant principles that he shared with the founders of the Bay Colony. This identity of fundamental precepts made refuting Williams difficult, since he accepted the basic religious convictions of his antagonists. Inasmuch as Williams was not a heretic, his break with Massachusetts and his final banishment took place over a period of years in which each side refined its views. Eventually both parties upheld these positions as part of a transatlantic debate regarding liberty of conscience in New and Old England. For the first time the lessons of America were interjected into a conflict confronted by the entire western world during the middle years of the seventeenth century.

BANISHMENT FROM MASSACHUSETTS BAY

In February, 1631, Roger Williams' arrival in America was duly noted by the Massachusetts Bay Colony Governor, John Winthrop, in his carefully kept diary. Winthrop described Williams as a "godly minister," and it is certain the young clergyman was welcome in the new colony at Boston.

There is good reason to believe that an important career was open to Roger Williams in New England. He was a man in his twenties whose promise and abilities had attracted the attention of one of England's most distinguished jurists, Sir Edward Coke. As a result of Coke's patronage, Williams won a scholarship to Cambridge University, where he graduated in 1627. A year after graduation he took holy orders as a minister of the Church of England. His first position, however, indicated an inclination to Puritanism. He accepted an appointment as chaplain in the home of Sir William Masham, whose family had wide connections in Puritan circles. The young minister's intellect and position were perfectly combined to attract attention in the Puritan community of the seventeenth century. Of special interest also were Williams' striking qualities as a person and his intense dedication to the service of God. Nearly all those who knew Williams were willing to testify to his magnetic qualities. Even his most bitter critics in later years openly acknowledged their affection and respect for him as an individual, and John Cotton, who denounced Williams' concept of religious liberty, admitted that his antagonist had received "stirring and useful gifts" from God. Further evidence of Williams' stature among the leading Puritan ministers is suggested by his participation in the discussions that took place before the massive Puritan migration to Massachusetts Bay. His opinions were highly valued and his prospects were surely unlimited. As Williams himself insisted, he might easily have "run the road of preferment" on either side of the Atlantic if it had been his desire.

A few days after his arrival in Massachusetts Williams was asked to join the congregation in Boston and serve for an indeterminate period as its teacher, an important ministerial appointment with primary responsibility for matters of faith and doctrine. John Wilson, the regular teacher of the Boston Church, was on the verge of returning temporarily to England; Roger Williams was asked to serve as his substitute. Wilson was having trouble with his recalcitrant wife who did not follow him to America during the original migration. In order to avoid the problem of broken homes, Wilson and others were instructed to return to the mother country and urge their wives to join them. The startled Boston Elders were rebuffed by Williams. He told them he would not serve a congregation that recognized the Church of England. Roger Williams, unknown to the Massachusetts colonists, had become a separatist.

The settlers of the Massachusetts Bay Colony were not separatists. Although they were similar to the Pilgrim community at Plymouth in believing that the Church of England was corrupt, unlike the Pilgrims the Massachusetts colonists did not repudiate that church entirely. The Massachusetts position held that there had always been a saving remnant of God's elect within the Anglican Church, which made it a true Church of God despite its corruptions. The Massachusetts brand of Puritanism did not demand or require renunciation. The colony's theologians believed that God required them to shun the errors of a false worship, but this did not mean they were obliged to denounce a church because it had some corruption. This position was an inheritance of the most important branches of English Puritanism. It also carried with it a large measure of political wisdom and expediency. A colony of the sort planned by the Massachusetts Bay Company required a good deal of outside assistance and a minimum of opposition. If the King or any powerful block of people were convinced the Bay Colony was composed of rigid separatists, the project would have been seriously threatened. The Massachusetts colony had no intention of inviting trouble from England because its enemies tried to misrepresent the settlement as a separatist undertaking.

Roger Williams' stand on this question was diametrically opposed

to that of the Massachusetts leaders. He believed that church agree-
ments and ordinances became unclean and debased in the sight of God
when they were corrupted by the inventions of men. For him God's
Church contained only the elect and was completely purged of every
natural and temporal imperfection. Since many of the ceremonies and
institutions of the Church of England distorted the word of God,
Williams was prepared to denounce its worship as erroneous and separate from it completely. In his desire for a church that was perfect
and pure, Williams followed the inner-spirit of New England Puritanism. The conflict over separatism grew out of the same impulse which
led to the founding of Massachusetts—a quest for perfection.

Separatism was only one of two disturbing issues with which
Roger Williams taxed the Bay Colony. The young minister also an-
nounced it was unlawful for the political officers of the settlement to
do anything to punish religious offenders. Of Williams' declarations
at this time, his opinion regarding the scope of the secular authority
was probably the more alarming. The colonists had not gone to America
with any notion of allowing religious dissent. Massachusetts was created to establish a correct and uniform worship of God. Consequently,
the civil magistrate, as in Europe, was expected to punish any breach
of God's commandments in the New World.

The basis of Williams' conclusions regarding the role of the civil
magistrate is of great importance in helping to understand his life
and ideas. Williams' thinking was essentially religious; the main problem of life, in his view, was the glorification of God. He believed that
God had set up two distinct levels of existence in this world: the
reality of nature and the reality of the spirit. A person participated in
both radically different worlds. Those whom God had chosen for
eternal life tried to live as free of the debasement of the natural world
as possible; those who remained unregenerate existed only in the reality
of what Williams called "cursed, rotten nature." The special obligation
of God's elect was to submerge the temptations of the natural world
and to glorify God by the pursuit of His spirit.

When Williams viewed the world he saw it in terms of a distinction between nature and the spirit. He gave these traditional Christian
concepts a radical twist by insisting on their absolute separation in
church and state. All the institutions of society, he felt, must reflect
this separation. As a result, the civil magistrate, who was created to
control the natural world, should not intrude upon the church. Since
the world "lies in wickedness, is a wilderness of sin," Williams ob-

served, it was alien to God's people. The government of the church was entirely spiritual; its methods of advocacy did not call for the weapons of the temporal world. It was this metaphysical separation between church and state that underlay the first controversies between Roger Williams and Massachusetts. As years went by, the theory would mature and he would extend it to support the proposition that every man should enjoy liberty of conscience.

After this first clash in Boston, Williams left quickly for Salem, where the illness of the congregation's teacher, the elderly Samuel Skelton, made an assistant necessary. Williams had earlier turned down a call to the Salem Church while still in England; his second invitation was probably not unexpected. The people of Salem were under the fiery leadership of John Endecott, one of the most explosive and determined of the colonists who came to Massachusetts. Led by Endecott, the Salem Church showed tendencies toward separatism and an intense desire for religious reformation that made Williams' call natural in spite of the altercation in Boston.

When the news of Williams' invitation to serve as assistant to Skelton arrived in Boston, Governor Winthrop and the magistrates were disturbed. The Governor responded by dispatching a letter to the Salem congregation. Williams, Winthrop reminded the people of Salem, was a separatist, and had expressed unorthodox opinions concerning the role of the civil officers in their relations with the church. The Governor and his colleagues wrote frankly that they could not understand why Salem had chosen Williams without consulting the government.

Aside from the information we have of the Winthrop letter to Salem, there is little else regarding this episode in the Williams story. It seems clear that the magistrates were determined to act against Williams before his ideas spread. Their concern did not arise out of malice but from a fear that his separatism was undiplomatic and that the ideas he expressed about the civil officers would rule out a uniform system of worship. No law or custom then existed which permitted the government to interfere in the affairs of an individual congregation. Nonetheless, the Governor made his protest on behalf of the government. Congregations, henceforth, would have to be more judicious in electing their officers. Debarring Williams at this time was an unofficial step and without legal sanction, but it did indicate the manner in which Massachusetts Bay was going to develop. At this juncture, we may presume, Williams found himself without support in Salem or desire to oppose the leaders of the colony. He decided to move south-ward to the Pilgrim settlement at Plymouth.

Roger Williams was probably content to live among the Pilgrims. He was attracted by the avowed separatism of the Plymouth congrega-tion. An added reason for his move to Plymouth may have been the opportunity it offered to study the Indians and their language. During his stay Williams made the most of his contact with the natives of the region. His bold respect for the Indians' dignity as men and his willing-ness to deal with them on a basis of equality won their lasting friend-ship. Of the relationship between the colonists and the Indians, Wil-liams declared: "Nature knows no difference between European and American in blood, birth, bodies, etc., God having of one blood made all mankind." He cautioned his fellow Englishmen:

> Boast not proud English of thy birth and blood,
> Thy brother Indian is by birth as good.
> Of one blood God made
> Him, and thee and all,
> As wise, as fair, as strong, as personal.

The Pilgrims received Williams graciously and welcomed him to their community. He was quickly admitted as a member of the church. The young minister also served as an assistant to the Plymouth teacher, Ralph Smith, himself an exile from Massachusetts.

Roger Williams did not remain long in Plymouth. According to William Bradford, the Plymouth Governor and its most authoritative historian, the new arrival was a "godly" and "zealous" person, but he was also "very unsettled in judgment." Williams again began to preach that the civil magistrate must not intervene in church affairs, an idea no less repugnant to the separatist Pilgrims than to their Calvinist co-religionists in Boston. Another irritant was his declaration that the colonists could not have title to the lands they held except by direct purchases from the Indians, the rightful owners. Williams prepared a treatise for the Governor and Council of the Plymouth plantation in which he charged that the Europeans could not claim American terri-tories solely on the basis of their Christianity or charters. He also sharply criticized the English monarchs, James I and Charles I, for granting charters and lands in North America without first buying these regions from the natives. As Williams saw it, the King could not give away what he did not own.

Since the Plymouth settlers were ready and willing to acknowledge every known Indian claim, Williams' protests seemed pointless. His charges caused controversy and discontent. The young minister and his ideas were proving as troublesome as in Boston.

Before conflicts in Plymouth reached an impasse, Williams returned abruptly to Massachusetts. In the fall of 1633 he was recalled by the Salem congregation to aid in the ministry of the dying Samuel Skelton. In order to avoid affronting the government, his position was unofficial. There can be little doubt that the forthright Williams went back to Massachusetts with misgivings. He was a man of God whose life and mind were committed to the driving spirit of religious reformation. He would compromise with no public evil that detracted from the purity of God's worship. "As a faithful watchman on the walls," Williams declared, he was obliged to "sound the trumpet and give the alarm" at any apprehension of evil, regardless of the consequences. If the evil he encountered involved the policies of Massachusetts Bay, Williams must have realized the government would not permit him to protest too loudly.

Soon Williams gained the attention of the magistracy again. The most important issues were his repeated complaints about the Indians' right to the land and his allegations that the English Kings were little better than robbers for attempting to give away a continent they did not possess.

Shortly after his reappearance in Salem, Williams raised the question of the lawfulness of the colonial settlements on the North American continent. Before leaving England, the Puritans agreed there could be no righteous claim to the lands they planted unless the Indians were compensated. But the Puritans did not reject the implication that their corporate charter and religion also provided a foundation for the occupation of Massachusetts Bay. The argument initiated by Williams was more theoretical than real, because the colonists took pains to buy the regions they settled from the Indians. Williams wanted them to do more. He brought out the treatise circulated earlier in Plymouth and sent it to the Boston government. He asserted that the colonial patent and the Christianity of the planters offered no right to any American territory unless the Indians were fully compensated.

Williams' protest and "loving reproof" respecting the rights of the Indians was a serious problem for the magistrates. They feared that his agitation over the colonial title to the soil questioned the validity of the Charter. Even in Plymouth the Pilgrims heard that the singular

Roger Williams "spoke dangerous words against the patent." Williams, of course, only wanted to denounce the presumption that the Charter of itself gave the settlers title to the New World. Nevertheless, the Puritan government was supersensitive on this point, because the Charter was a key to its independent plans in America and a shield against hostile critics in the mother country. In fact, at the very moment that Williams assailed the government for failing to deal righteously with the Indians, the colony was under attack at home and abroad. A number of towns and freemen were distressed with the arbitrary practices of the Winthrop government on matters of taxation and other items, while in England the colony faced stubborn and powerful foes who were taking steps to destroy the Massachusetts experiment. It was unfortunate for Williams that the entire period of his residence in Massachusetts was fraught with external danger to the colony. This threat gave his protests a meaning and significance that transcended the borders of the New World province.

Williams' treatise on the Indian lands boldly defamed the English Kings, James I and Charles I. Williams complained that James I was guilty of a "public lie" for pretending in the Massachusetts Charter that he was the first European monarch to discover North America. When Charles I upheld the validity of his father's false claims, Williams implied he was little better than the anti-Christian devils of the Book of Revelation. A third allegation was in much the same vein: Williams objected to the use of the term "Christendom" in the Massachusetts Charter, because it suggested that Western Europe was a Christian society. These charges were typical of Williams, and prompted John Cotton, in exasperation, to say he was a "haberdasher of small questions," noting that "even Christendom itself is an unsavory word to him." Williams accused both James I and Charles I of blasphemy for putting the label of "Christendom" on the different nations of Western Europe. "The civil state of nations being merely and essentially civil," he reasoned, "cannot (Christianly) be called Christian states." According to Williams, the only truly Christian state is that of God's elect; a blanket endorsement of all the countries and peoples of Europe as "Christendom" was an improper association of a spiritual distinction with the secular world. It was this supposedly unholy mixing of nature and grace which inspired his diatribe against the Kings of England.

After learning of the government's worry about his treatise, Williams wrote to Governor Winthrop disclaiming any disloyal intentions.

His complaint, he explained, had been written only for the private information of the magistrates in hope of forestalling illegal occupation of Indian territories. Williams denied any wish to press the matter further and Winthrop was satisfied with his disclaimers. The government promptly reassured Williams of its intention to buy any legitimate claims the Indians possessed in the colony. Williams' conscience was sated. As a gesture of reconciliation, he offered to destroy any part of his treatise that was deemed offensive, a promise he probably kept since no copy of the work exists today.

Although the controversy over the Indian lands and the Charter was quietly resolved, the episode was clearly indicative of problems that Roger Williams stirred up in Massachusetts. His pronouncement regarding the unrighteousness of taking the Indians' land was a provocative embarrassment for the magistrates; the accusation of sinful conduct struck deep and was not easily forgotten. In making his charges, the young minister showed himself to be an uncontrollable man of conscience, whose passionate and precipitant actions might disrupt the peace of the settlement. The government was particularly disconcerted by his outspoken separatism as well as the uncomplimentary statements about England's rulers. To insult the reigning King and his father with allegations of lying and blasphemy intensified the many dangers then threatening the colony from the mother country. The importance of Williams' activities reverberated beyond the limits of Massachusetts.

A powerful and determined opposition to the colony developed around two principal figures in England, Sir Ferdinando Gorges and Charles I. The hostility of Gorges to Massachusetts stemmed from his past colonizing activities in the region and because the Massachusetts Bay Company superseded his patents in the area of Massachusetts. Gorges' earlier attempts to found a colony in New England were failures. His cherished plans for a feudal paradise in America were now further shattered by the successful Massachusetts plantation. In addition, Gorges still held claims to much of northern New England, and he harbored sensible fears of the expansive Puritans.

Early in 1633 the Massachusetts government became aware of the deep-seated antagonism of the English Crown to the colony. The Puritan exodus to Massachusetts had been large, and a number of the King's counsellors recommended an end to this migration. Even more ominous was the elevation of William Laud, an enemy of the Puritans, to be Archbishop of Canterbury, the primate of the Anglican Church.

Laud's policies directly contradicted the Puritan quest for a more austere church service, and his search for uniformity of worship resulted in the persecution of Puritan dissenters. The new Archbishop's demand for conformity might reach out to America and endanger the Massachusetts colony.

Initial attacks on Massachusetts came in the form of judicial procedures aimed at rescinding the Massachusetts Charter. The colony's critics, encouraged by Sir Ferdinando Gorges, instituted legal proceedings against the patent, charging that the settlers wanted to throw off allegiance to the mother country. Soon thereafter, the King, urged by William Laud, stopped ten ships loaded with passengers leaving for New England. At the same time, Governor Winthrop learned that the Privy Council had inquired regarding the whereabouts of the Massachusetts Charter and had requested that it be returned to England for examination and defense. Matthew Cradock, one of the original sponsors of the colony who did not settle in America, informed Winthrop that the Privy Council wanted the patent; he asked Winthrop to comply before the Privy Council struck out against the friends of Massachusetts in London. Governor Winthrop, perplexed about what to do, decided to evade the issue. He notified Cradock that the Charter could not be sent to England until the General Court of Massachusetts met again in several months. Temporarily Winthrop delayed, but the passage of time only fired the wrath of those seeking to ruin the Massachusetts experiment.

In April, 1634, the government in Boston received news that put the colony in extreme peril. If God had promised his saints a permanent utopia in New England "from where they shall move no more," as predicted in 1630, the prophecy now appeared doomed. Governor Winthrop acquired a copy of the King's order establishing a Royal Commission with complete power to regulate the plantations and resolve colonial problems. The hostile nature of the Commission was indicated by the choice for Chairman, Archbishop William Laud. With sweeping authority from the Crown, Laud might be able to undo in one stroke all that Winthrop and the settlers had accomplished in five years of labor and sacrifice.

How to respond to this danger was a question of the greatest magnitude. Officially, Massachusetts expressed its willingness to accept the King's new regulatory agency as a token of respect and subordination to the mother country. In a formal address to the Commission, the Bay Colony's rulers professed their loyalty and firm adherence to the church and state of England. "We dare not question your Lordship's proceedings," they said to Laud, "if in anything we have offended His Majesty and your Lordship, we humbly prostrate ourselves at the footstool of supreme authority." While the magistrates were thus officially meek and pliable before an intractable foe, they took a very different unofficial course of action. The General Court and local authorities throughout Massachusetts began to ready their defenses. The colonial government, speeded on by Winthrop, ordered construction of fortifications in the major ports, inhabitants of military age were given arms, and the militia reserves were brought to the point of combat readiness. A last step was the organization of a military committee by the General Court. This body, composed of the leading men of the settlement, took control over the extensive efforts to secure the colony; it was specifically empowered "to make either offensive or defensive war." Massachusetts prepared for any eventuality.

The Laud Commission demonstrated its antagonism to Massachusetts by appointing Sir Ferdinando Gorges Governor General of New England. The region was divided into new jurisdictions and the independent authority of the Massachusetts Bay Company eliminated. It was decided to send Gorges and a strong force of soldiers to New England in order to reduce the Puritans to a sense of obedience. A ship to carry the expedition to America was completed late in the spring of 1635. Happily for the Puritans, the vessel proved unseaworthy and the project was postponed. Before another force could be assembled, the mother country entered into a period of civil war, which made the Massachusetts venture wholly impractical. These circumstances saved the colony from a severe and unequal struggle.

Events at home and abroad brought the conflicts with Roger Williams to a crisis. Besides the threats from England, the colonial government was fearful of hostile incursions from the Indians and French on the frontiers of New England. Reacting to these dangers, the General Court decided to require everyone to take an oath of loyalty to the government. Williams objected vehemently and publicly to the oath; his behavior now seemed insufferable. Williams' scruples about the Freeman's Oath grew out of the same religious convictions that characterized his earlier protests. He argued that a civil officer could not force an oath upon the people because an oath was an act of worship, and many of the settlers, being unregenerate, should not be compelled to participate in a religious ceremony. In Williams' estimation, the name of God should be invoked only by the elect, and this necessarily ruled out the mass of men. "An oath does remain religious," he said, "though conversant about civil matters." If every person in Massachusetts were made to swear an oath, this would be a perversion of God's worship and an "indignation of the Most High."

The governor and assistants hastily met with Williams and confronted him with the latest in his series of public declarations against their policies; the Salem minister seemed out of tune with the system of life developing in Massachusetts Bay. A conference of church and state officials was called to discuss Williams' opinions and refute them. The ministers of the colony were convinced that Williams was wrong and the secular authorities had every right to tender oaths to the population on civil matters. With the animosity of Bishop Laud passing across the Atlantic and the entire populace being readied for a defense of their "liberties," Williams had taxed the forbearance of the magistrates beyond limit; they considered his obstreperous pronouncements seditious. In view of the situation, it is surprising Williams was not expelled from Massachusetts without further deliberation. The reason the government held back was the intervention of the clergy in his behalf, especially the most famous minister in Massachusetts, John Cotton.

It was not unusual in Massachusetts for the government to consult with the ministers in difficult cases under consideration, particularly those dealing with religion. The ministers were significant personages in Puritan Massachusetts and were called upon in almost all controversies for their advice and guidance. The clergy was best educated to lead the colony into a more intimate communion with the ways of God. Its role was often crucial.

John Cotton was the most prominent minister in Massachusetts. His influence derived from his achievements as a scholar and his extraordinary gifts in the pulpit. At Cambridge, Cotton's brilliant record as a student resulted in his rapid rise in academic circles; he became fellow and then dean of Emmanuel College, the intellectual center of English Puritanism. Cotton's eminence was later enhanced by his position as rector of St. Botolph's Church in Boston, Lincolnshire, an important ministerial appointment. It did not take long for Cotton to transform the town and surrounding community into a widely admired example of Puritan reformation, and his appeal as a preacher and pastor soon affected the outlying county and the nation. Cotton preached the farewell sermon before the great Massachusetts migration to America in 1630. Three years later, persecuted and hunted by Archbishop William Laud, he escaped to New England.

Cotton's relations with Roger Williams were paradoxical. Since he was the chief spokesman of the Massachusetts orthodoxy after 1638 and probably its major architect, his reputation is that of a thoroughly one-dimensional exponent of the New England Way. This interpretation is confirmed by Cotton's role in later years as the Massachusetts author who defended the colony against Williams' attacks and denounced liberty of conscience. Ironically, although Cotton's writings may be used by the historian to explain why Roger Williams was thrown out of Massachusetts, these works were written after the event. They contain evidence that at the time Cotton sympathized with Williams and took his part to stave off his certain banishment in 1634.

John Cotton had known Williams in England, and the two men participated in discussions concerning the proposed plantation in the New World. Cotton remembered Williams' piety, soundness of doctrine, and eagerness to devote his life to God's truth. Even if the Salem minister was difficult and dangerous, the problem was simply one of misguided conscience. There was no personal antagonism between them; as saints of God they both understood that positive conviction was a virtue, not a fault. In Williams' case, however, Cotton was willing to admit the protestor was much too zealous and forward. In consequence, he chose to intervene in Williams' behalf, explaining that the young minister's statement about the loyalty oath was a matter of conscience and on this account more suitable for ministerial disputation than civil prosecution. Once shown the error of his ways, Cotton suggested, Williams would cease his factious behavior.

Upon the convening of a meeting to decide what to do with Williams, Cotton recalled: "I presented with the consent of my fellow elders and brethren a serious request to the magistrates that they would be pleased to forbear all civil prosecution against him, till we ourselves (with our churches) had dealt with him in a church way." Deferring to Cotton and the other ministers and hopeful that the clergy might be able to tame the irrepressible cleric, the government agreed to postpone proceedings against the irksome Williams. Governor Thomas Dudley, who had been elected to replace John Winthrop, warned the ministers they were deceived if they thought Williams would ever learn anything from them. "And what will you do," he asked Cotton, "when you have run your course and found all your labor in vain?" Cotton answered for the rest that they expected a better outcome.

The government's delay in acting against Roger Williams did not signal its willingness to drop the matter of the oath and wipe his slate clean. Salem misunderstood. In the summer of 1634 Samuel Skelton died after a lengthy illness, and the congregation chose Williams as its teacher in spite of his difficulties with the colonial authorities. The magistrates were unhappy that the rebel minister was chosen for such an important church office while he stood in contempt of the government's policies. They asked the Salem congregation to reconsider his election.

Before this problem could be resolved, Williams and his personal crisis with the government moved to a conclusion. On July 8, 1635, he was summoned to Boston and accused of harboring many "dangerous opinions." The General Court had passed a number of statutes aimed at establishing a uniform system of worship throughout the colony. At the same session of the General Court, the ministers were queried to "consider how far the magistrates are bound to interpose for the preservation of that uniformity and peace of the church." Contrary to the traditional impression of the Puritan Age in Massachusetts as an era of static conformity, of a well-marked-out system of church and state from the beginning, these requests indicate that the planters were not sure of the precise form their New World experiment would take. The system evolved as a product of their ideas and experience, developing slowly as the situation permitted. The men of Massachusetts were not all of one stamp; there was room for differences of opinion, even on the most sensitive questions. Hence the desire of the government to have the churches and the people advise on the relationship of church and state. Williams probably replied to the government's request for advice from the ministry. He answered as might be expected, reasserting his old argument that the civil magistrate should not interfere in any church matter, because the mixing of temporal and religious jurisdictions was ungodly. This objection, coming on top of the still unresolved issue of the Freeman's Oath, was viewed as open rebellion.

The magistrates met and discussed Williams' career in the colony and his most recent ideas. His viewpoints were adjudged "erroneous and very dangerous." Williams' selection as teacher of the Salem congregation was decried as a "great contempt of authority," and the young minister as well as the congregation were given the opportunity to study the conflict and relent. Both were cautioned "either to give satisfaction to the court, or else to expect sentence."

Although Williams and Salem were given time to weigh their positions and relationship to the government, another contest arose which precipitated the banishment of Roger Williams from Massachusetts. Salem had proffered a petition to the General Court calling for a grant of land in the Marblehead Neck region of the plantation, an area which the town claimed as part of its boundaries. The Salem petition was rejected by the magistrates. The people of Salem were informed that their selection of Williams as teacher of the congregation precluded a favorable reception of their request.

Affronted and angry, the congregation, doubtless spurred on by Williams, wrote to the other churches of the colony publicly admonishing the government for its unwarrantable decision in refusing the Salem petition. The townsmen denied the validity of this judgment and expressed their concern that the magistrates had presumed to interfere with the autonomy of their independent congregation. The magistrates were not laggard in suppressing the Salem protest before it spread. At its first succeeding meeting, the General Court unseated all the deputies from Salem "for their lies sent to the general churches, wherein they have exceedingly reproached and vilified the magistrates and deputies of the General Court . . . ." The legislators voted that the town should remain unrepresented until it disclaimed the circular letter to the churches. When John Endecott exploded in disapproval of the General Court's actions, he was arrested and imprisoned for contempt. The Boston Church, meanwhile, put added pressure on Salem by sending along a public notice admonishing the congregation for electing and supporting Williams. This letter, signed by John Cotton and two elders, asserted that Williams' activities were beginning to disturb the peace of the community. The Boston note also stated that Williams' concept of the role of the civil officers would make it impossible to restrain religious dissent and would allow the churches of the colony to erupt into heresy.

Under the combined pressures of the magistrates and the ministry, the Salem congregation gave way. It agreed to seek an accommodation with the General Court that would fully satisfy any complaints. Even the indomitable Endecott, after a stinging protest, surrendered. John Winthrop inscribed in his diary that Endecott "acknowledged his fault and was discharged." But Williams remained stubborn. Although ill, he informed the Salem congregation that the single course left open in these circumstances was to refuse to have any associations with the rest of the churches in the Commonwealth, a break the people would not take. Realizing that the town was on the verge of capitulation, Williams withdrew from the congregation and resigned his office of teacher. He was prepared to face the wrath of the magistrates by himself if necessary and to be expelled from Massachusetts as an acknowledgment of the "truth of God."

Having humbled Salem, the General Court proceeded to initiate conclusive steps against the "heady" and "violent" Williams. He had been warned to give satisfaction or expect sentence. On October 7, 1635, the General Court of Massachusetts gathered to consider the case of Roger Williams. At the request of the legislators a number of ministers were present and were asked to participate in the debate.

Governor John Haynes opened the proceedings with a text from scripture, indicting Williams as a vexatious and headstrong person who was overthrowing the peace of the community. "Now I beseech you, brethren," he read, "mark them which cause divisions and offenses contrary to the doctrine you have learned; and avoid them."

The Salem minister was accused of stirring up quarrels among the churches of Massachusetts and attempting to dissolve the allegiance of the people to the magistrates by false allegations of injustice and oppression. Williams refused to retract any of his opinions and actions. At this point, the ministers offered to dispute with him in a final effort to convince him of the error of his ways. Williams chose to debate immediately, instead of waiting a month as suggested. Thomas Hooker of Newtown, soon to be a founder of Connecticut, was selected to confute the young cleric. Williams did not recant. As a result, with all the ministers and magistrates convinced he was an intransigent and beyond redemption, he was ordered to leave Massachusetts Bay. The official banishment declared Roger Williams had "broached and divulged divers new and dangerous opinions against the authority of the magistrates." Since he would not compromise, Williams was directed to "depart out of this jurisdiction."

A DEBATE IN NEW AND OLD ENGLAND

Warned by John Winthrop in January, 1636, that the government was preparing to ship him back to England, Williams fled southward in the midst of winter and founded a colony along the shores of Narragansett Bay. His first resolution was to put the bitter experience in Massachusetts behind him and focus all his energies on the struggling Providence plantation. In a frank message to his friend Winthrop, he spoke of an eagerness to lay aside past conflicts and press forward in the arduous work of building a colony. Despite this desire to forget and begin anew, the banishment remained one of Williams' constant preoccupations in the wilderness. The experience went too deep to be left behind. Besides, the young minister believed there was greater meaning in the incident than the personal hurt he had suffered. Because of his struggle with Massachusetts, Williams believed he saw more clearly than ever the proper relationship of church and state. Roger Williams became an advocate of the separation of church and state and liberty of conscience.

Almost simultaneously with his declaration to Winthrop of a wish to forget the past, he began to pepper his New England correspondents with letters and statements discussing the circumstances of his banishment and presenting his radical ideas about the nature of church and state. The Massachusetts settlers, in turn, especially Winthrop and Cotton, defended the government's decision in expelling Williams. The Salem minister had been a dangerous troublemaker, they implied, and the colony was more cohesive and secure with him gone. In contemplating Williams' novel pronouncements about church and state, the Bay leaders saw further confirmation of the wisdom of his banishment.

These exchanges between Williams and Massachusetts were not public and would never have gained notoriety except for the prolonged civil war that convulsed England between 1640 and 1660. The religious and political strife of the mother country had a direct impact on the American colonies. The Rhode Island settlement, which had been started without charter or legal right, seemed particularly endangered by the turmoil in England. In consequence, Roger Williams was authorized to act as Rhode Island's agent, and he returned to England after a fourteen-year absence. He was sent as emissary of the Narragansett colony in hope of obtaining legal sanction from the revolutionary government of England. The settlers feared that without such official recognition their unorthodox colony would not be safe from enemies on both sides of the Atlantic.

When Roger Williams arrived in London in 1643 England was facing the greatest religious and political contentions of its history. Under the leadership of Parliament, the King had been defeated in a bloody war and virtually deposed; the hated Episcopal system, so generally loathsome to the Puritans, was on its deathbed. Puritanism had triumphed, and a new order of reformation waited to be born.

In September, 1642, Parliament ordered the dissolution of the Episcopal hierarchy of bishops and archbishops. The principal goal of Parliament was to eliminate Anglicanism as an arm of the monarchy and to reconstruct the Church of England under Parliament's control. As yet there was little concern over the precise form of the religious settlement, regarding either matters of structure or doctrine. Parliament wanted to dominate whatever religious system it authorized to replace Anglicanism.

The course of events during the civil war drastically narrowed the range of alternatives open to Parliament. In order to win the war against the King, Parliament was obliged to seek the support of Scotland and its armies. In return, the Scots were determined to gain the establishment of their religious order, Presbyterianism, as the official worship of the entire British Empire. Moreover, an agreement known as the "Solemn League and Covenant" pledged the English and Scottish allies to bring the different parts of the nation into "the nearest conjunction and uniformity in religion." Since Presbyterianism was already established in Scotland, this seemed to commit Parliament to the religious system of its most important ally.

Without the support of Scotland, Parliament would have found it almost impossible to defeat Charles I. Its willingness to commit the nation to a reformed religious structure in close harmony with Scotland's Presbyterianism was logical and understandable. Once victory was in sight the Puritan elements in Parliament disintegrated into a host of factions, each with its own purposes and plans. Although no one religious group was dominant, the Presbyterian party was the most numerous and influential.

This dissension was not unexpected, but it was dangerously disconcerting in the middle of a civil war. In the hope that a consensus might be worked out among the most active Puritan groups, Parliament authorized the convocation of an assembly of clergymen in the summer of 1643 to agree upon a religious and doctrinal settlement for the kingdom. This was the famous Westminster Assembly that met in London over a period of six years. Most members of the Assembly wanted to recognize Presbyterianism as the official church of the British Empire. A Presbyterian establishment would have resulted in a uniform doctrine based on Calvinism and a church government of elected bodies of presbyters, synods, and a general assembly. A few Episcopalians favorable to a church hierarchy of bishops and archbishops attended the first sessions, but they withdrew immediately after the King denounced the meeting. Another minority group in the Westminster Assembly was known as the Independents. This faction shared the Calvinist predisposition of the Presbyterian majority, but they were unwilling to accept any religious superstructure above the individual churches. They advocated a religious system in which each congregation was completely independent, subject only to the supervision of elected elders and to the fundamental principles of Christianity. Communion among the Independent Churches should be voluntary. This group, although only a handful in the Westminster Assembly, had support in the army and an articulate following in the House of Commons.

Hopelessly outvoted in the Assembly, the Independents were in a hazardous situation. At first it appeared almost assured that the Presbyterian majority would prevail. The Independents were determined to forestall such a settlement, and they began an energetic campaign in the Assembly against the Presbyterian leanings of the assembled divines. At the same time, knowing that Presbyterianism might be adopted anyway, the Independents tried to lay the groundwork for a future accommodation between the two chief Puritan factions. They began to emphasize the similarities in doctrine between the parties. Since they were so close in basic doctrine and differed mostly over the nature of church government, was it possible that the Independent congregations might be permitted to coexist along with a Presbyterian establishment? The Independents had no wish to recommend a similar indulgence for other dissenting churches—they were not yet spokesmen for religious freedom—but they were anxious that a way be found for their denomination to survive the apparently inevitable triumph of Presbyterianism in England.

This split among the Puritan clerics was made public in 1644 by the publication of *An Apologeticall Narration,* a short work written by five Independent ministers participating in the Westminster Assembly, Thomas Goodwin, Philip Nye, Sidrach Simpson, Jeremiah Burroughs, and William Bridge. These "dissenting brethren" openly acknowledged their dedication to an Independent system of autonomous congregations. Their Congregationalism was offered as the godly "middle-way" between the extremism of the radical sects and the rigid authoritarianism of the Presbyterians. The apologists, however, were also sedulous to make clear the broad circle of agreement that unified the major parties in the Westminster Assembly. It is commonly known, they declared, that "in all points of doctrine . . . our judgments have still concurred with the greatest part of our brethren. . . ." The pamphlet urged the contending ministers to follow the Independent example and yield the "utmost latitude" to men of similar consciences; in other words, in the event of defeat, the Independent dissenters were pleading for their own toleration.

Despite its concentration on the similarities between the Calvinist factions and its guarded sentiment in favor of religious toleration, the *Apologeticall Narration* created a sensation. Instead of soothing the contentious ministers, it caused a multitude of outcries from all sides. One of the most spectacular attacks came from Roger Williams.

By the time he returned to England Roger Williams was a confirmed advocate both of the separation of church and state and of a coherent philosophy of liberty of conscience. These beliefs were not newly born on his arrival in London but had been nurtured by his religious convictions and personal experience in being expelled from Massachusetts Bay. He believed the principles so dearly bought and tested in New England were eminently suitable for the mother country as well. Williams sensed that the Puritan Revolution had destroyed the uniformity of the Anglican Church and that no succeeding religious establishment could ever encompass the numerous sects that were appearing. The differences between the most important Calvinist factions, the Presbyterians and Congregationalists, were already so hardened and embittered that they could not be reconciled without either mutual tolerance or the use of force. Williams recommended the precepts of his New World colony of Rhode Island as a solution to the Old World's deepening religious crisis.

While in Massachusetts Bay Williams had questioned the intervention of the civil government in the affairs of the church. Williams doubted that God required the civil government to play any role in enforcing His religious injunctions; he saw no reason for the government in Boston to enforce obedience to the first table of the Ten Commandments, which prescribed the obligations due between men and God. Later this clash with the Bay Colony broadened into an issue of greater significance. When Williams recalled the problems involved in his banishment he saw the conflict as an unmistakable instance of religious persecution in which he was not allowed freedom of worship. Moreover, his first probing doubts about the relations of church and state, which had centered on particular issues such as the loyalty oath, the Ten Commandments, and the Massachusetts Charter, now became the vital problem of the "civil magistrate dealing in matters of conscience and religion." The real issue in his banishment, Williams implied, was his general attack on the intervention of the civil officers in any matter of conscience.

According to Roger Williams, secular officers could have no responsibility in matters of worship because church and state were very different in their origins and wholly divergent in their duties. In his most famous work, *The Bloudy Tenent of Persecution* (1644), Williams wrote that "all civil states with their officers of justice in their respective constitutions and administrations, are proved essentially civil and, therefore, not judges, governors or defenders of the spiritual or Christian state and worship." The nature of the state was completely secular, reasoned Williams, because it was ordained by God to regulate the material concerns of men. In contrast, the Kingdom of Christ was completely different. God's realm was totally spiritual and admitted of no worldly interests or material concerns. As a result, the secular officer, rooted in the natural world, had no part to play in the fulfillment of God's will.

Adding to his views regarding the separation of church and state, Williams also commented on the membership of each. He asserted that the composition of the two societies was so radically different as to mandate complete separation. Williams saw the civil government as the representative of the natural world; it included every person in its jurisdiction irrespective of his religion or faith. The Church of God was the antithesis of the state. It was made up only of the elect and was required to purge itself of every worldly and natural impurity. Considering their distinct memberships and divergent duties, Williams concluded, church and state had to be totally separated.

A logical if not inevitable extension of Williams' doctrine of separation of church and state was his belief that all men were entitled to absolute freedom of worship. In the aftermath of his expulsion from Massachusetts Bay, Williams strove to demonstrate that liberty of conscience was an integral part of God's design and should not be denied to any person. Forced worship, he proclaimed, "stinks in God's nostrils."

If church and state were constituted as distinct and unconnected institutions, it was a natural corollary that liberty of conscience must be given to everyone. Without the coercive power of the state, dissent would be uncontrollable and legitimized. Williams also argued that the church itself had no right to force anyone's conscience; it could not supplant the coercive authority of the civil government. He explained that a true church was a tender and merciful society, which did not require the use of force in calling people to the service of the Lord. Possibly influenced by the Baptists, Williams envisioned a religious organization that was held together by a mutual and voluntary striving after God's law. In this regard, the weapons of the church were patterned after the benevolent Christ of the New Testament, who rejected the armaments of the natural world in achieving His ends. True belief was not compatible with physical compulsion. Quite the contrary. The Christian Church does not persecute, wrote Williams, "no more than a lilie does scratch the thornes, or a lamb pursue and tear the wolves, or a turtle dove hunt the hawkes and eagles. . . ." The only weapons of God's Church are spiritual.

The vigorous books which Williams published were written with the English situation in mind. He was eager to present his own unusual ideas on how to resolve the critical problems raised by the proliferation of sects during the Puritan Revolution. His books were also a frontal assault on the Bay Colony and the brand of persecution he claimed to have sampled there. He assailed the Massachusetts system of church and state as oppressive and destructive of the peace and well-being of the community. By intended implication, Williams suggested that if New England's Congregationalism were adopted in the mother country it would "blow up all religion, all civility, all humanity."

The acute crisis in English religious life made certain that Williams' striking publications would find a wide and responsive audience. His *Bloudy Tenent* became one of the most noted books of the Puritan Revolution. One thing was evident: No one was indifferent to what Roger Williams had to say.

Williams' participation in the acrimonious disputes of the English civil war placed the Massachusetts Bay Colony in a difficult position. The New England settlers were part of the larger party of English Puritans who were called Independents by contemporaries. The Massachusetts planters and the English Independents were identical in their commitment to a Congregational system of church organization and a theology based on Calvinism. When the revolution in England unseated Charles I and toppled the hated Episcopacy of Archbishop Laud, the question of a church establishment created division in the Puritan ranks. The Scottish allies of Parliament and the English Presbyterians seemed to win a majority in the Westminster Assembly. They wanted to suppress dissent and establish Presbyterianism as the official Church of England. In contrast, the Independent minority struggled for Congregationalism and an acceptance of a mutual policy of tolerance among the major Puritan factions. It was on the latter point that Roger Williams added a new dimension to the contest. In describing his treatment by the Massachusetts government, Williams alleged that the American Congregationalists were intolerant and would brook no dissent from their New World orthodoxy. Using this evidence, the English Presbyterians were able to denounce the Independent appeal for toleration as hypocritical and insincere, citing the case of Roger Williams as indicative of the real feelings of the Independents in America and England.

This should not be taken to mean that the Presbyterians welcomed Williams' provocative statements about the nature of religious liberty and order. For them his ideas were virtually blasphemous; they wanted no settlement that permitted more than one worship. Whatever might be the opinions of Williams, wrote Robert Baillie, a leading Scottish representative at the Westminster Assembly, "Liberty of conscience and toleration of all or any religion is so prodigious an impiety that this religious Parliament cannot but abhor the very naming of it." Still the Presbyterians were heartened by Williams' publications. His statements about Massachusetts convinced them of the duplicity of the Independent plea for tolerance. George Gillespie, a Presbyterian member of the Assembly, offered the Massachusetts persecution of Williams as proof that were the Independents "able to root out the Presbyterians and their way, and could find civil authority inclinable to put forth the coercive power against it, whether in that case they would not say that the magistrate may suppress it by a strong hand, if it cannot be otherwise repressed." The New World experience of Roger Williams thus became an element in the English debate over the organization of a national church.

A Massachusetts response to Roger Williams was dictated by compelling reasons. Many of the Bay Colony's leaders were irritated and outraged that Williams had characterized his banishment as an instance of religious persecution. In their view, he had been thrown out solely for civil reasons, because of his irresponsible and seditious campaign against the Boston government. Another factor calling for a refutation was the political and religious situation in the mother country. The Presbyterians' use of Williams' charges was harmful to the struggle for

Congregationalism and the effort of the Independents to secure toleration for themselves. Furthermore, a Presbyterian establishment in England might becloud the future growth of Congregationalism in America. Williams' allegations had to be rebutted. In the process of rebuttal
the Massachusetts Puritans were forced to define their stand on the
most delicate problems of religious liberty and order.

The task of replying to Roger Williams fell upon John Cotton.
Cotton's role in the polemics with Williams was brought about under
mysterious circumstances. Shortly after Williams' banishment he cor-
responded with Cotton and asked him to comment on the proper relationship of church and state. Cotton responded in a lengthy letter
that was published without his authorization after Williams arrived in
London. Williams disclaimed any part in the appearance of the Cotton
letter, and then went on to assail Cotton and the Massachusetts Puritans for not sanctioning absolute freedom of worship. Provoked by
Williams' assault, Cotton replied in several works that put Williams
and himself in the midst of a profound transatlantic debate over church-
state relations.

John Cotton's major work in reply to Roger Williams was clearly
cognizant of the great issues raised by the Puritan Revolution. After
more than a century of religious turmoil initiated by Henry VIII's
break with Rome, English society had to reconstitute its church order.
Cotton's principal rejoinder to Williams, *The Bloudy Tenent, Washed,
and made white in the bloud of the Lambe* (1647), centered forcefully
on the key issues in dispute.

> "How far liberty of conscience ought to be given to those that
> truly fear God?
> "And how far restrained to turbulent and pestilent persons, that
> not only raze the foundations of godliness, but disturb the civil
> peace where they live?
> "Also, how far the magistrate may proceed in [enforcing] the
> duties of the First Table [of the Ten Commandments]?"

The Boston teacher wanted his replies to summarize the New England
reconstruction of church-state relations and offer it as a model for the
divided factions of the mother country.

The basis of John Cotton's views about the nature of church-state
relations was his firm conviction that the truth of God was revealed
and might be made clear to any fair-minded person. Starting from
this conviction, Cotton asserted the only religious freedom that God

granted mankind was an absolute freedom to accept His will. There was no religious liberty other than the right to choose the single, revealed truth. "It is no impeachment of church liberty," Cotton remarked, "but an enlargement of its beauty and honour to be bound by strict laws and holy commandments, to observe the pure worship of God, and to be subject to due punishment for gross violation of the same." To Cotton it was a distortion of the truth to pretend God ever proposed that men be allowed to select error and falsehood.

Cotton also contended that it was the fate of man in this world to be continually tempted with the choice between good and evil. Man's obligation was to select the good. He denounced Williams' appeal for toleration as an open sanction of every imaginable religious abomination and a bid for the protection of error. Such a plea was insane. Tolerance would foster the spread of error and result in its victory over the truth. Cotton saw no safe compromise with falsehood. So wide a difference exists between truth and error, he argued, that the competition of both, considering man's weakness, would lead to the triumph of lies and falsehood. Cotton could find no middle-ground between working for religious purity and permitting total corruption.

Church and state must not be divided into completely separate societies, Cotton insisted. He admitted the church was a merciful institution that could not utilize the weapons of the secular world, but he saw no reason why the civil government should not be enjoined to encourage God's truth. Cotton suggested that it was the religious responsibility of the civil officer to sustain the church and promote its progress. As an institution deriving from God, the state must not stand aside and be neutral while erroneous and heretical ideas overpowered the church. The civil magistrate, Cotton maintained, should act as a "nursing father" of the Church of God. Besides sponsoring the church, the civil officers were bound to forbid error. If this seemed a negative contribution to the glory of God, it was still a service of the greatest importance. Cotton argued that prosecution stopped the spread of dissent and comforted the saints of God in their daily striving after God's commandments. Moreover, the prevention of wickedness might act as a "wholesome medicine" and bring those who misunderstood or remained stubborn to correct their ways and walk firmly on the paths laid out by God.

Something of the Calvinist legacy in New England Puritanism appears repeatedly in Cotton's refutation of Roger Williams. The Calvinist feared an ever-present, omnipotent, vengeful God who demanded everlasting glorification and took retribution for ungodliness. The fear of God's punishment in this world inclined some Puritans to seek uniformity of worship, even at the price of physical coercion. "For if the church and the people of God fall away from God," Cotton explained, "God will visit the city and country with public calamity, if not captivity, for the church's sake." A nation that tolerated spiritual decadence kindled God's wrath and invited untold misfortune. In contrast, when a state was closely in tune with God's commands and fulfilled the divine pattern of life, God visited that country with well-being and prosperity. Persecution was, therefore, desirable because "the punishments executed upon false prophets, and seducing teachers, do bring down the showers of God's blessings upon the civil state." It appeared to Cotton that God had united church and state with indestructible ties of mutual self-interest.

Cotton also declared Williams mistaken in his notions regarding the strictly civil functions of government. Although the magistrate's principal responsibility was to control the outward man and not his spiritual life, this did not rule out religious duties for the secular officer. By their very purpose civil laws were supposed to serve the best interests of the community, and there was nothing better for the people than religion. For this reason, civil laws and the secular officers should play a part in the religious life of the commonwealth. "That is a civil law whatsoever concerns the good of the city, and the propulsing of the contrary," Cotton informed his readers. "Now, religion is the best good of the city, and, therefore, laws about religion are truly called civil laws . . . for the promoting and preserving of that good of the city." Furthermore, Cotton affirmed, the essential purpose of society was the glorification of God. Believing this, it was absurd to think the state should exist with no concern for the church. "The world and all societies of it are for the church," related Cotton. "The world would not subsist but for the church, nor any country in the world, but for the service of the church." The religious idealism and spiritual earnestness of some Puritans fortified their demand for a unified church and state. They feared the religious purity of the nation could not be achieved without state intervention.

In responding to Roger Williams and upholding Massachusetts Bay, John Cotton confirmed the traditional value of a union of church and state and the propriety of forcing all men to conform to an established faith. Implicitly, however, he seemed to sustain the Presbyterian judgment that every denomination, including the Independents, should conform to a single church. Since it appeared that Presbyterianism would be established by Parliament, Cotton's debate with Williams gave aid and comfort to the enemies of the Independent Congregationalists in the mother country. In order to meet the embarrassment of the apparently different approaches to the problem of toleration among the New and Old World Congregationalists, Cotton was obliged to elaborate on his views regarding the timing and applicability of civil prosecution for religious reasons. He said that Roger Williams had not been persecuted in New England and went on to explain that dissenters were to be suppressed under special circumstances and only in limited cases.

Cotton denied that Williams had been banished from Massachusetts because of his faith. Williams' actions and opinions, Cotton protested, made him a "public enemy of the country, and, as such a one, in due order to be cast out of it." Cotton maintained that the opposition of the magistrates to Williams was not persecution. Persecution meant the punishment of an individual for religious beliefs that were correct and true in the sight of God. This was not the situation with Roger Williams. His ideas were clearly erroneous and were rejected by the unanimous vote of the most important clergymen in Massachusetts. In strict accordance with biblical procedures, Williams was punished after repeated warnings and admonitions. It was his stubborn behavior, his refusal to accede to the truth, his "sin against the very light of his own conscience," intoned Cotton, which led to his exile. If anyone persecuted Roger Williams, it was the young man himself, who would not receive the word of God after it had been revealed to him by the combined ministry of the Bay Colony. "How can I be said to maintain persecution for the cause of conscience," Cotton concluded, when it was obvious Williams invited banishment by his recalcitrance? The punishment of a "culpable" and "damnable" person can never be equated with religious persecution.

Indicating some irritation with Williams' heated charges, Cotton asserted that his antagonist saw each act of the civil magistrate as an instance of religious persecution. His eyes are bloodshot, Cotton remonstrated, and because of it he sees everything around him as "red and bloody." Cotton observed that the New England Way did not envisage the punishment of dissenters for every act of religious non-conformity. Massachusetts offered a wide measure of practical toleration to men of differing consciences provided their opinions were not boisterous and dangerous to the peace of the colony. Only seditious and turbulent beliefs were restrained in Massachusetts. Secondly, Cotton contended that the American Congregationalists expected religious conformity only in fundamental articles of the Christian faith; outside of this, they were willing to tolerate other beliefs and professions. A third possibility of toleration was necessity: During certain periods in history mutual compromise between conflicting faiths was a pragmatic alternative to bloodshed and violence. "I easily acknowledge sometimes a necessity of a state toleration," he admitted, in those instances, as in the mother country, when the suppression of dissent is impossible. Thus refining and delimiting his views, John Cotton tried to counteract the philosophy of Roger Williams and systematize the orthodoxy of the New England Puritans.

John Cotton's re-evaluation of the many-sided problems of church and state came at a time when no one could be blind to the growing multiplicity of the sects. It became virtually impossible to expect one system of worship to satisfy most people in the revolutionary world of seventeenth-century England. Still the values and customs of the past could not be hastily abandoned. Unity of church and state and religious uniformity might yet be attained within the framework of fundamental Christian doctrines and an honest recognition that men who shared these common principles should not fight over non-essentials. This approach permitted a limited amount of mutual toleration and rejected the visionary propositions of men like Roger Williams. It satisfied Congregationalists in Old and New England during the first critical years of the Puritan Revolution.

Roger Williams did not passively accept John Cotton's defense of the Bay Colony. In his vigorous rebuttal he continued to militate for the separation of church and state and complete liberty of conscience. Williams added to his major sources of authority—religion and theology—arguments drawn from history and practicality. In each of his provocative publications he refurbished his ideas and presented them in the hope of influencing the final religious settlement in the mother country.

In his larger theological and intellectual orientation, Roger Williams followed the Calvinist tradition. His quest for religious perfection underlay the radical ideas he developed about the nature of church and state. As a Calvinist, he accepted the doctrines of the natural depravity of man, predestination, and eternal election. He shared the overall theological perspectives of his antagonists, and this made him difficult to contend with, whether in Boston or London. With considerable irony Williams used his Calvinism to repudiate his co-religionists' supposed intolerance regarding freedom of worship.

Calvinist that he was, Roger Williams was painfully aware of man's corrupt nature and the tendency of every man, including God's saints, to commit sinful acts. Williams surmised that it was unwise to prosecute men for their shortcomings because even a sinner, despite his failings, might still be among God's elect. For this reason, no one could ever be certain another person's conscience was either right or wrong, for God may be "very pleased to hide" from His own chosen people. Since God's decrees were often inscrutable and difficult to discern, this should temper the severe punishments meted out for religious causes. "And if God hide from His, from any," he asked, "who can discover?" Before any man's conscience was forced, Williams cautioned the persecutor to consider whether he did not without knowing hunt "the life of my Saviour and the blood of the lamb of God."

Williams was also forthright in drawing from the Calvinist doctrinal system implications that seemed to fortify his tolerant beliefs. Pressing the logic of predestination to an unusual conclusion, he reasoned that since the issue of salvation was already decided, God wanted men to be free to fulfill their spiritual destinies. Why compel a man to believe, when he was unable? Forced worship implied that an individual had free will to choose among religious alternatives and that he would honor God after he was reprimanded and coerced. Williams found these traditional assumptions in conflict with the basic principles of Calvinism. When Cotton answered that religious liberty would permit men to indulge their sinful natures and make their corruptions worse, Williams remained firm in his conviction that God alone could change a man's faith. The will to believe, he said, came only from God.

A further deduction from the ideas of John Calvin came from the principle of election. The elect, regardless of their failings, could never fall from salvation. Just as the damned were beyond hope of redemption, the saints of God could never be subverted and led into mortal sin. For this reason, Williams pointed out, it was presumptuous to interfere with spiritual errors by the use of force and violence. "As I spoke unto the argument of the impossibility of the perishing of any of God's elect, so here the use of such an argument is . . . but to condemn the over-wise and over-busy heads and hands of men, adding their inventions to God's appointments," Williams concluded. "Whereas God's number of living and dead are certain . . . and notwithstanding all other means in the world used by men as helps and hindrances, yet His . . . holy end shall not be disappointed, but fulfilled." In his campaign to propound the idea of absolute religious freedom, Roger Williams gave a radical turn to the precepts of Calvinism.

In a final and sweeping attack on the theological presuppositions of his adversaries, Williams denied that the Old Testament might serve as a pattern for a contemporary religious settlement. The issue was critical. In planning a religious establishment for the English nation, each faction sought the creation of a Christian state that would cultivate and preserve the purity of God's worship. In this respect, the New Testament could not be an effective model for an integrated religious and political commonwealth. The New Testament recorded an era when Christianity had been a persecuted minority struggling for survival in a hostile world; its implications for a Puritan orthodoxy that united church and state were conflicting. In contrast, the Old Testament offered the best example of the orthodoxy contemplated by the Puritans in America and in the mother country. The prescriptions of the Mosaic law provided a complete replica for the union of church and state and the punishment of religious non-conformists.

Virtually every critic of Roger Williams relied on the Old Testament to justify his opinions. John Cotton was no exception. In developing laws for the Massachusetts plantation, Cotton worked out a judicial system that rested heavily on precedents of the Mosaic heritage that were particularly harsh in the prosecution of religious offenders. Contradicting Williams, he asserted the moral validity and universal force of the Mosaic laws. "It is moral equity that blasphemers, apostates, and idolaters, seducing others, should be put to death," pronounced Cotton. While he admitted the ceremonial obligations of the Jews were no longer binding on Christians, Cotton believed parts of the Mosaic heritage were still compulsory, especially the Ten Commandments.

Meeting the challenge imposed by the Old Testament to the acceptance of his ideas, Williams utilized a method of biblical criticism known as "typology." The use of typology in interpreting the Bible was not unique to Williams; most theologians, including John Cotton, invoked the typological approach in expounding certain sections of the Old Testament. Few scholars, however, were ready to use the technique in order to reject the validity of the judicial system of the Jews.

Typology was employed in theological studies as a method of developing the relationships that exist between the two revelations in the Old and New Testaments. Instead of assuming the two parts of the Bible were inconsistent, most commentators believed the Old Testament served as a precursor of the New. People and events of the Old Testament were understood to foretell the coming of Christ. A good example was the story of Jonah, in which Jonah was said to typify Christ, and his imprisonment in the belly of a whale foretold Christ's descent into Hell and resurrection. Unlike other theologians, Williams applied this typological method to all sections of the Old Testament. He claimed the punishments enjoined under the Mosaic statutes for religious crimes were meant by God to foreshadow the far more terrible spiritual torment that Christ would decree for those who failed to gain salvation. Williams went further and believed the land of Canaan as well as the Hebrew experience should not be a model for the political and religious life of the seventeenth century. This was particularly true of the Mosaic laws, including those relating to church and state, which "were proper and peculiar to that land and people of Israel." The church order of the Jews must never be taken as a literal pattern for any other epoch.

Not only did Williams try to show the way religious freedom was consistent with the fundamental principles of Christianity, but he was hopeful of demonstrating the practical necessity of this policy. Arguments from necessity and history provide a major source of authority in his debate with John Cotton and other proponents of religious conformity and the union of church and state.

In face of the multiplicity of denominations, Williams advised accepting every sect on the basis of freedom and equality. Intrusion of the civil officers into this plurality of belief would be futile. "And must we raise up such tumults, such tragedies, and fill the face of the world with streams of blood," he questioned, "about the Christian magistrate reforming religion, establishing religion, killing the heretic, blasphemer, idolater, seducer? . . ." Williams concluded liberty of conscience was the only means of preventing untold and senseless bloodshed. "There is no other prudent, Christian way of preserving peace in this world but by the permission of different consciences," he wrote. In Williams' opinion, toleration and peace were inseparably joined together.

In presenting his proposal for complete religious freedom, Williams trod hard on a cherished notion of many ages. The traditional commitment to the union of church and state and religious uniformity was still powerful. Adding support to these customary beliefs was the idea that any breach in the unity of church and state, as Cotton related, would bring havoc to the entire nation. God would not tolerate an impious country. Williams rejected this supposition. He held that freedom of many worships would in no way endanger the community. He used the record of history to bear out the validity of his contention. "I have in the experience of many ages observed the flourishing prosperity of many cities, commonwealths, and nations, where no sound of Christ has come," Williams pointed out. The prosperity and safety of the pagan civilizations in ancient times were never dependent on the holiness of their peoples; likewise, the economic success of Holland, a contemporary experiment in toleration, indicated religious freedom was not hazardous. To say as Cotton did that church and state must fall together, Williams contended, was to misrepresent the lessons of past and present.

Uniting church and state, Williams said, made the civil magistrate the final arbiter of true and false conscience. This situation was dangerous to religious purity, because the secular officer might not always select the proper worship. History revealed that civil governments of the world were never in agreement about the commandments of God. Indeed, there were many occasions when secular rulers avidly promoted patently false beliefs. The history of England in the sixteenth and seventeenth centuries showed that it was folly to allow the government to regulate spiritual life. As different sets of religious beliefs and practices replaced one another in the years following Henry VIII's break with Rome, each claimed to be the true holy pattern. Williams remembered the upheavals in England's religious life that came after the death of Henry VIII. In view of this distressing past, he contended the civil ruler was not a reliable yardstick for religious truth. "Who knows not how easy it is to turn and turn and turn again whole nations from one religion to another?" Williams asked. The precedent of England's established religion "changing as fashions" showed it was foolhardy to permit the civil magistrate to judge the validity of any man's faith.

Williams also pointed out the questionable results of forcing religious conformity. "The civil sword may make a nation of hypocrites and anti-Christians," he observed, "but not one Christian." While he confessed the threat of punishment might achieve outward conformity, it could never bring inward submission to the will of God, the essence of a Christian life. "What a woeful proof hereof have the nations of the world given in all ages," he wrote. In reality, force produced the opposite of conviction, because persecution only confirmed a man in his disbelief and made him a martyr.

With these arguments based on practicality and history, Roger Williams ended his great debate with John Cotton. Time would prove that uniformity after the pattern of the past was impossible. The floodgates of tradition had been opened in the Puritan Revolution, and the outpourings of religious diversity could never again be contained.

If we are now to judge Roger Williams and John Cotton, it must be within the context of an era long since gone. Today the controversy has a clarity it did not possess at the time. Roger Williams, praised and glorified in retrospect, proposed radical and revolutionary concepts in a period of unparalleled questioning of accepted institutions and traditions. Only today do his ideas appear unmistakably fitting and correct, because the accumulation of years has made them familiar and acceptable. For most contemporaries the views of John Cotton were probably as persuasive, particularly in America. Cotton wanted to offer his civilization a resolution of its unique religious problems. If his recommendations were not lasting, they invited an adjustment to the divergent forces unleashed by the Protestant Reformation and the Puritan Revolution. John Cotton's monument was the untold influence of his thought on the New England way of life.

part one

THE EXPULSION OF
ROGER WILLIAMS FROM
MASSACHUSETTS BAY

Shortly after Williams settled at Providence, Rhode Island, probably in 1636 and 1637, he started a correspondence with the leaders of the Bay Colony about the relationship of church and state and the nature of religious freedom. Implicitly, in these letters and later in his published works, he suggested that his banishment was an example of religious persecution. The spokesmen for Massachusetts, however, vigorously maintained that the troublesome Williams had been thrown out of the colony for civil reasons. As John Cotton explained, Roger Williams became a "public enemy" of Massachusetts because his erratic behavior disturbed the peace and good order of the community. The many conflicting interpretations of Williams' banishment throughout the years are in reality a repetition of the original opinions of Williams and Cotton and their contemporaries.

Among the sources relating to the banishment of Roger Williams, none is richer in detail or more authoritative than the diary of John Winthrop. Winthrop's record is remarkable for the moderation with which he recorded the events relating to Williams and the many dangers facing the colonists at home and abroad.

Neither Winthrop nor John Cotton initiated the public controversy with Roger Williams. One of Cotton's private letters to Williams, on the subject of religious freedom and Williams' banishment, was published without authorization shortly after Williams arrived in London. Williams quickly replied in a book entitled *Mr. Cottons Letter Lately Printed, Examined and Answered* (1644). Williams' rejoinder called for a response from the scholarly Cotton. Each of Cotton's contributions to the public discussion attempted to justify Williams' expulsion from Massachusetts, reject the charge of persecution, and uphold the reputation of the Bay Colony.

source 1

Governor John Winthrop's Diary *

John Winthrop

[February 5, 1631]. The ship *Lyon*, Mr. William Peirce, master, arrived at Nantasket. She brought Mr. [Roger] Williams (a godly minister), with his wife . . . about twenty passengers, and about two hundred tons of goods. She set sail from Bristol, December 1. She had a very tempestuous passage. . . .

[April 12, 1631]. At a court holden at Boston (upon information to the governor, that they of Salem had called Mr. Williams to the office of a teacher), a letter was written from the court to Mr. Endecott to this effect: That whereas Mr. Williams had refused to join with the congregation at Boston, because they would not make a public declaration of their repentance for having communion with the churches of England, while they lived there; and, besides, had declared his opinion, that the magistrate might not punish the breach of the Sabbath, nor any other offense, as it was a breach of the first table [of the Ten Commandments]; therefore, they marvelled they would choose him without advising with the council; and withal desiring him, that they would forbear to proceed till they had conferred about it. . . .

[September 25, 1632]. The governor [John Winthrop], with Mr. [John] Wilson, pastor of Boston, and the two captains, etc., went aboard the *Lyon*, and from thence Mr. Peirce carried them in his

---

* The sources included in this book have been modernized in the interest of clarity of expression. Changes have been made in the original texts which eliminate typographical errors, contractions, abbreviations, outmoded use of italics, punctuation, capitalization, and spelling, and unnecessary Biblical citations. Every effort has otherwise been made to retain the exact meaning and character of the documents.

James Savage, ed., *The History of New England from 1630 to 1649 by John Winthrop, Esq. First Governour of the Colony of Massachusetts Bay* (Boston: 1825-1826), 2 vols. *Passim.*

shallop to Wessaguscus [Weymouth]. The next morning Mr. Peirce returned to his ship, and the governor and his company went on foot to Plymouth, and came thither within the evening. The governor of Plymouth, Mr. William Bradford (a very discreet and grave man), with Mr. Brewster, the elder, and some others, came forth and met them without the town, and conducted them to the governor's house, where they were very kindly entertained, and feasted every day at several houses. On the Lord's day there was a sacrament [Lord's Supper], which they did partake in; and, in the afternoon, Mr. Roger Williams (according to their custom) propounded a question, to which the pastor, Mr. Smith, spoke briefly; then Mr. Williams prophesied [lectured]; and after the governor of Plymouth spoke to the question; after him the elder; then some two or three more of the congregation. Then the elder desired the governor of Massachusetts and Mr. Wilson to speak to it, which they did. When this was ended, the deacon, Mr. Fuller, put the congregation in mind of their duty of contribution; whereupon the governor and all the rest went down to the deacon's seat, and put into the box, and then returned. . . .

[January 17, 1633]. The governor [John Winthrop], having intelligence from the east, that the French had bought the Scottish plantation near Cape Sable, and that the fort and all the ammunition were delivered to them, and that the Cardinal [Richelieu], having the managing thereof, had sent some companies already, and preparation was made to send many more the next year, and divers priests and Jesuits among them—called the assistants to Boston, and the ministers and captains, and some other chief men, to advise what was fit to be done for our safety, in regard the French were likely to prove ill neighbors . . . .

[February 22, 1633]. The ship *William*, Mr. Trevore, master, arrived at Plymouth with some passengers and goods for the Massachusetts Bay. . . .

By this ship we had intelligence from our friends in England, that Sir Ferdinando Gorges and Captain [John] Mason [who also had claims in New England] . . . had proffered a petition to the lords of the Privy Council against us, charging us with many false accusations; but, through the Lord's good providence, and the care of our friends in England . . . their malicious practice took not effect. The principal matter they had against us was the letters of some indiscreet persons among us, who had written against the [Anglican] church government in England, etc., which had been intercepted . . . .

[May, 1633]. By these ships [newly arrived from London] we understood, that Sir Christopher Gardiner, and Thomas Morton, and Philip Ratcliff (who had been punished here for their misdemeanors), had petitioned to the King and Council against us, (being set on by Sir Ferdinando Gorges and Captain Mason . . .). The petition was of many sheets of paper, and contained many false accusations, . . . accusing us to intend rebellion, to have cast off our allegiance, and to be wholly separate from the church and laws of England; that our ministers and people did continually rail against the state, church, and bishops there, etc. . . .

[November, 1633]. The ministers in the Bay and Sagus did meet, once a fortnight, at one of their houses by course, where some question of moment was debated. Mr. [Samuel] Skelton, the pastor of Salem, and Mr. Williams, who was removed from Plymouth thither (but not in any office, though he exercised by way of prophecy [lecturing]), took some exception against it, as fearing it might grow in time to a presbytery or superintendency, to the prejudice of the churches' liberties. But this fear was without cause; for they were all clear in that point, that no church or person can have power over another church; neither did they in their meetings exercise any such jurisdiction, etc. . . .

[December 27, 1633]. The governor [John Winthrop] and assistants met at Boston, and took into consideration a treatise, which Mr. Williams (then of Salem) had sent to them, and which he had formerly written to the governor and council of Plymouth, wherein, among other things, he disputes their right to the lands they possessed here, and concluded that, claiming by the King's grant, they could have no title, nor otherwise, except they compounded with the natives. For this, taking advice with some of the most judicious ministers (who much condemned Mr. Williams' error and presumption), they gave order, that he should be convented at the next Court, to be censured, etc. There were three passages chiefly whereat they were much offended: 1, for he charged King James to have told a solemn public lie, because in his patent [to the Massachusetts Bay Company] he blessed God that he was the first Christian Prince that had discovered this land; 2, for that he charged him and others with blasphemy for calling Europe Christendom, or the Christian world; 3, for that he did personally apply to our present King, Charles [I], these three places in the [New Testament] Revelations, viz., [*blank*].

Mr. [John] Endecott being absent, the governor wrote to him to let him know what was done, and withal added divers arguments to confute the said errors, wishing him to deal with Mr. Williams to retract the same, etc. Whereto he returned a very modest and discreet answer. Mr. Williams also wrote to the governor, and also to him and the rest of the council, very submissively, professing his intent to have been only to have written for the private satisfaction of the governor, etc., of Plymouth, without any purpose to have stirred any further in it, if the governor here had not required a copy of him; withal offering his book, or any part of it, to be burned.

At the next Court he appeared penitently, and gave satisfaction of his intention and loyalty. So it was left, and nothing done in it. . . .

[January 24, 1634]. The governor [John Winthrop] and council met again at Boston, to consider of Mr. Williams' letter, etc., when, with the advice of Mr. [John] Cotton and Mr. Wilson, and weighing his letter, and further considering of the aforesaid offensive passages in his book (which being written in very obscure and implicative phrases, might well admit of doubtful interpretation), they found the matters not to be so evil as at first they seemed. Whereupon they agreed, that, upon his retraction, etc., or taking an oath of allegiance to the King, etc., it should be passed over. . . .

[April 1, 1634]. Order was taken for ministering an oath to all house keepers and sojourners, being twenty years of age and not freemen . . . .

[July, 1634]. Mr. Humfrey and the lady Susan, his wife, one of the Earl of Lincoln's sisters, arrived here. He brought more ordnance, muskets, and powder, bought for the public by monies given to that end; for godly people in England began now to apprehend a special hand of God in raising this plantation, and their hearts were generally stirred to come over . . . . Likewise, Mr. Humfrey brought certain propositions from some persons of great quality and estate (and of special note for piety), whereby they discovered their intentions to join with us, if they might receive satisfaction therein. It appeared further, by many private letters, that the departure of so many of the best, both ministers and Christians, had bred sad thoughts in those behind of the Lord's intentions in this work, and an apprehension of some evil days to come upon England. Then it began now to be apprehended by the archbishops, and others of the council, as a matter of state, so as they sent out warrant to stay the ships, and to call in our patent; but, upon petition of the shipmasters, (attending how beneficial this plantation was to England) in regard of the Newfoundland fishing, which they took in their way homeward, the ships were at that time released. But Mr. Cradock (who had been governor [of the Massachusetts Bay Company] before the government was sent over [to America]) had strict charge to deliver in the patent; whereupon he wrote to us to send it home. Upon receipt of his letter, the governor [Thomas Dudley] and council consulted about it, and resolved to answer Mr. Cradock's letter, but not to return any answer or excuse to the [King's] council at that time. . . .

[July 9, 1634]. Mr. Cradock wrote to the governor and assistants, and sent a copy of the council's order, whereby we were required to send over our patent. Upon long consultation whether we should return answer or not, we agreed, and returned answer to Mr. Cradock, excusing that it could not be done but by a General Court, which was to be holden in September next. . . .

[August 2, 1634]. Mr. Samuel Skelton, pastor of Salem, died . . . .

[September 18, 1634]. At this court were many laws made against tobacco and immodest fashions, costly apparel, etc., as appears by the records; and £600 raised toward fortifications and other charges, which were the more hastened, because the *Griffin* and another ship now arriving with about two hundred passengers and one hundred cattle, . . . there came over a copy of the [royal] commission granted to the two archbishops [including William Laud] and ten others of the [King's] council, to regulate all plantations, and power given them, or any five of them, to call in all patents, to make laws, to raise tithes and portions for ministers, to remove and punish governors, and to hear and determine all causes, and inflict all punishments, even death itself, etc. This being advised from our friends to be intended specially for us, and that there were ships and soldiers provided, given out as for the carrying the new governor, Captain Woodhouse, to Virginia, but suspected to be against us, to compel us, by force, to receive a new governor, and the discipline of the Church of England, and the laws of the commissioners, occasioned the magistrates and deputies to hasten our fortifications, and to discover our minds each to other . . . .

[November 27, 1634]. It was likewise informed, that Mr. Williams of Salem had broken his promise to us, in teaching publicly against the King's patent, and our great sin in claiming right thereby to this country, etc., and for usual terming the churches of England anti-Christian. We granted summons to him for his appearance at the next Court. . . .

[April 30, 1635]. The governor [Thomas Dudley] and assistants sent for Mr. Williams. The occasion was, for that he had taught publicly, that a magistrate ought not to tender an oath to an unregenerate man, for that we thereby have communion with a wicked man in the worship of God, and cause him to take the name of God in vain. He was heard before all the ministers, and very clearly confuted. Mr. Endecott was at first of the same opinion, but he gave place to the truth. . . .

[June 16, 1635]. By a letter from the Lord Say, and report of divers passengers, it was certified to us, that Captain Mason and others, the adversaries of this colony, had built a great ship to send over the general governor [Ferdinando Gorges], etc., which, being launched, fell in sunder in the midst.

It appeared likewise, by a copy of a petition sent over to us, that they had divided all this country of New England, viz. between St. Croix in the east, and that of Lord Baltimore, called Maryland, into twelve provinces, disposed to twelve in England, who should send each ten men to attend the general governor coming over; but the project [did] not [take] effect. The Lord frustrated their design. . . .

[July 8, 1635]. At the General Court, Mr. Williams of Salem was summoned, and did appear. It was laid to his charge, that, being under question before the magistracy and churches for divers dangerous opinions, viz. 1. that the magistrate ought not to punish the breach of the first table [of the Ten Commandments], otherwise than in such cases as did disturb the civil peace; 2. that he ought not to tender an oath to an unregenerate man; 3. that a man ought not to pray with such, though wife, child, etc.; 4. that a man ought not to give thanks after the sacrament nor after meat, etc.; and that the other churches were about to write to the church of Salem to admonish him of these errors; notwithstanding the church [at Salem] had since called him to [the] office of a teacher. Much debate was about these things. The said opinions were adjudged by all, magistrates and ministers (who were desired to be present), to be erroneous, and very dangerous, and the calling of him to office, at that time, was judged a great contempt of authority. So, in fine, time was given to him and the church of Salem to consider of these things till the next General Court, and then either to give satisfaction to the Court, or else to expect the sentence; it being professedly declared by the ministers (at the request of the court to give their advice) that he who should obstinately maintain such opinions (whereby a church might run into heresy, apostacy, or tyranny, and yet the civil magistrate could not intermeddle) were to be removed, and that the other churches ought to request the magistrates so to do . . . .

[July 12, 1635]. Salem men had proffered a petition, at the last General Court, for some land in Marblehead Neck, which they did challenge as belonging to their town; but, because they had chosen Mr. Williams their teacher, while he stood under question of authority, and so offered contempt to the magistrates, etc., their petition was refused till, etc. Upon this the church of Salem wrote to other churches, to admonish the magistrates of this as a heinous sin, and likewise the deputies; for which, at the next General Court, their deputies were not received until they should give satisfaction about the letter. . . .

[August 16, 1635]. Mr. Williams, pastor of Salem, being sick and not able to speak, wrote to his church a protestation, that he could not communicate with the churches in the Bay; neither would he communicate with them, except they would refuse communion with the rest; but the whole church was grieved herewith. . . .

[September 1, 1635]. At this Court, Mr. Endecott made a protestation in justification of the letter formerly sent from Salem to the other churches against the magistrates and deputies, for which he was committed; but, the same day, he came and acknowledged his fault, and was discharged. . . .

[October 7, 1635]. At this General Court, Mr. Williams, the teacher at Salem, was again convented, and all the ministers in the Bay being desired to be present, he was charged with the said two letters—that to the churches, complaining of the magistrates for injustice, extreme oppression, etc., and the other to his own church, to persuade them to renounce communion with all the churches in the Bay, as full of anti-Christian pollution, etc. He justified both these letters, and maintained all his opinions; and being offered further conference or disputation, and a month's respite, he chose to dispute presently. So Mr. Hooker was appointed to dispute with him, but could not reduce him from any of his errors. So, the next morning, the Court sentenced him to depart out of our jurisdiction within six weeks, all the ministers, save one, approving the sentence; and his own church had him under question also for the same cause; and he, at his return home, refused communion with his own church, who openly disclaimed his errors, and wrote an humble submission to the magistrates, acknowledging their fault in joining with Mr. Williams in that letter to the churches against them, etc. . . .

[January, 1636]. The governor [John Haynes] and assistants met at Boston to consider about Mr. Williams, for that they were credibly informed, that, notwithstanding the injunction laid upon him (upon the liberty granted him to stay [in Massachusetts] till the spring) not to go about to draw others to his opinions, he did use [the delay in his expulsion] to entertain company in his house, and to preach to them, even of such points as he had been censured for; and it was agreed to send him into England by a ship then ready to depart. The reason was, because he had drawn above twenty persons to his opinion, and they were intended to erect a plantation about the Narragansett Bay, from whence the infection would easily spread into these churches (the people being, many of them, much taken with the apprehension of his godliness). Whereupon a warrant was sent to him to come presently to Boston, to be shipped [to London], etc. He returned answer (and divers of Salem came with it), that he could not come without hazard of his life, etc. Whereupon a pinnace was sent with commission to Captain Underhill, etc., to apprehend him, and carry him aboard the ship, . . . but, when they came at his house, they found he had been gone three days before; but whither they could not learn.

He had so far prevailed at Salem, as many there (especially of devout women) did embrace his opinions, and separated from the churches, for this cause, that some of their members, going into England, did hear the ministers there, and when they came home the churches here held communion with them. . . .

source 2

A Reply to John Cotton

Roger Williams

This letter I acknowledge to have received from Mr. Cotton (whom for his personal excellencies I truly honor and love). Yet at such a time of distressed wandering among the barbarians that, being destitute of food, of clothes, of time, I reserved it (though hardly, amidst so many barbarous distractions), and afterwards prepared an answer to be returned.

In the interim, some friends being much grieved that one publicly acknowledged to be godly and dearly beloved [i.e., Williams] should yet be so exposed to the mercy of an howling wilderness, in frost and snow, etc., Mr. Cotton, to take off the edge of censure from himself [for Williams' banishment], professed both in speech and writing that he was no procurer of my sorrows.

Some letters then passed between us in which I proved and expressed that if I had perished in that sorrowful winter's flight, only the blood of Jesus Christ could have washed him from the guilt of mine.

His final answer was: "Had you perished, your blood had been on your own head; it was your sin to procure it, and your sorrow to suffer it."

Here I confess I stopped, and ever since suppressed my answer, waiting if it might please the Father of mercies more to mollify and soften, and render more humane and merciful, the ear and heart of that (otherwise) excellent and worthy man [John Cotton] . . . .

Though I humbly desire to acknowledge myself unworthy to be beloved, and most of all unworthy of the name of Christ and to be beloved for His sake, yet since Mr. Cotton is pleased to use such an

Roger Williams, *Mr. Cottons Letter Lately Printed, Examined and Answered* (1644), *The Writings of Roger Williams*, 6 vols. (Providence, R.I.: Narragansett Club Publications, 1866-74), I, 31-32, 36, 37, 40-45, 53-54, 111-12.

affectionate compellation and testimonial expression to one so afflicted and persecuted by himself and others (whom for their personal worth and godliness I also honor and love), I desire it may be seriously reviewed by himself and them, and all men, whether the Lord Jesus be well pleased that one beloved in Him should (for no other cause than shall presently appear) be denied the common air to breath, in and a civil cohabitation upon the same common earth? . . .

Secondly, I observe his charge against me for not harkening to a two-fold voice of Christ: first, of the whole church of Christ with me.

Unto which I answer according to my conscience and persuasion. I was then charged by office with the feeding of that flock, and when in the apprehension of some public evils the whole country professed to humble itself and seek God, I endeavored (as a faithful watchman on the walls) to sound the trumpet and give the alarm; and upon a fast day, in faithfulness and uprightness (as then and still I am persuaded), I discovered eleven public sins for which I believed (and do) it pleased God to inflict and further to threaten public calamities, most of which eleven (if not all) they seemed to assent unto, until afterward in my troubles the greater part of that church was swayed and bowed (whether for fear of persecution or otherwise) . . . .

After my public trial and answers at the General Court, one of the most eminent magistrates [John Winthrop] (whose name and speech may by others be remembered) stood up and spoke:

"Mr. Williams," said he, "holds forth these four particulars.

"First, that we have not our land by patent from the King, but that the natives are the true owners of it, and that we ought to repent of such a receiving it by patent.

"Secondly, that it is not lawful to call a wicked person to swear, to pray, as being actions of God's worship.

"Thirdly, that it is not lawful to hear any of the ministers of the [Anglican] parish assemblies in England.

"Fourthly, that the civil magistrate's power extends only to the bodies and goods and outward state of men, etc."

I acknowledge the particulars were rightly summed up, and I also hope that as I then maintained the rocky strength of them to my own and others' consciences' satisfaction, so (through the Lord's assistance) I shall be ready for the same grounds, not only to be bound and banished, but to die also in New England, as for the most holy truths of God in Christ Jesus.

"Yea but," said he, "upon those grounds you banished yourself from the society of the churches in these countries."

I answer, if Mr. Cotton means my own voluntary withdrawing from those churches resolved to continue in those evils and persecuting the witnesses of the Lord presenting light unto them, I confess it was my own voluntary act. Yea, I hope the act of the Lord Jesus sounding forth in me, a poor despised ram's horn, the blast [of] which shall in His own holy season cast down the strength and confidence of those inventions of men in the worshipping of the true and living God. And, lastly, His act in enabling me to be faithful in any measure to suffer such great and mighty trials for His name's sake. But if by banishing myself he [Cotton] intends the act of civil banishment from their common earth and air, I then observe with grief the language of the Dragon in a lamb's lip. Among other expressions of the Dragon are not these common to the witnesses of the Lord Jesus rent and torn by his persecutions? "Go now, say you are persecuted, you are persecuted for Christ, suffer for your conscience. No, it is your schism, heresy, obstinacy; the Devil has deceived you, you have justly brought this upon you, you have banished yourself, etc." Instances are abundant in so many books of martyrs, and the experience of all men, and therefore I spare to recite [more examples] in so short a treatise. . . .

Now to the ground from whence my prejudice might arise: he [Cotton] professes my banishment proceeded not with his counsel or consent. I answer, I doubt not but what Mr. Cotton and others did in procuring my sorrows was not without some regret and reluctancy of conscience and affection. . . . Yet to the particular that Mr. Cotton consented not, what need he, being not one of the civil court? But that he counselled it (and so consented), besides what other proof I might produce, . . . I shall produce a double and unanswerable testimony.

First, he publicly taught and teaches (except lately Jesus Christ taught him better) that body-killing, soul-killing, and state-killing doctrine of not permitting, but persecuting, all other consciences and ways of worship but his own in the civil state, and so, consequently, in the whole world, if the power or empire thereof were in his hand.

Secondly, as at that sentence divers worthy gentlemen dared not concur with the rest in such a course [of banishment], so some that did consent, have solemnly testified, and with tears, since to myself confessed, that they could not in their souls have been brought to have consented to the sentence, had not Mr. Cotton in private given them advice and counsel, proving it just and warrantable to their consciences. . . .

Thirdly, for myself, I acknowledge it a blessed gift of God to be enabled to suffer and so to be banished for His name's sake. And yet I doubt not to affirm that Mr. Cotton himself would have counted it a mercy if he might have practiced in Old England what now he does in New, with the enjoyment of the civil peace, safety, and the protection of the state.

Or, should he dissent from the New English churches and join in the worship with some other . . . would he count it a mercy to be plucked up by the roots, him and his, to endure the losses, distractions, miseries that do attend such a condition? The truth is both the mother and the daughter, Old and New England, for countries and governments, are lands and governments incomparable; and might it please God to persuade the mother to permit the inhabitants of New England, her daughter, to enjoy their conscience to God after a particular Congregational way, and to persuade the daughter to permit the inhabitants of the mother, Old England, to walk there after their conscience. . . . I conceive Mr. Cotton himself, were he seated in Old England again, would not count it a mercy to be banished from the civil state. . . .

Upon these considerations how can Mr. Cotton be offended that I should help (as he calls them) any zealous souls, not against the mighty ordinances of the Lord Jesus, but to seek after the Lord Jesus without halting? Yea, why should Mr. Cotton or any desirous to practice reformation kindle a fire of persecution against such zealous souls, especially considering that themselves, had they so inveighed against bishops, common prayers, etc. in Edward VI his days, had been accounted as great heretics in those reforming times as any now can be in these. Yet would it have been then, and since has it been, great oppression and tyranny to persecute their consciences; and still will it be for them to persecute the consciences of others in Old or New England.

How can I better end than [as] Mr. Cotton does, by warning that all that will not kiss the Son (that is, hear and embrace the words of His mouth) shall perish in their way? And I desire Mr. Cotton and every soul to whom these lines may come seriously to consider in this controversy, if the Lord Jesus were himself in person in Old or New England, what church, what ministry, what government he would set up, and what persecution he would practice toward them that would not receive Him? . . .

An Answer to *The Bloudy Tenent*

John Cotton

Mr. Williams sent me about a dozen years ago [1636?] (as I remember) a letter, penned (as he wrote) by a prisoner in Newgate, touching persecution for conscience sake, and entreated my judgment of it for the satisfaction of his friend. I was not willing to deny him any office of Christian love and gave him my poor judgment in a private letter. This private letter of mine he has published in print after so many years, and there with a refutation of it. If my letter was orthodox and tending to satisfaction and edification, why did he refute it? If corrupt and erroneous (especially if bloody), why did he publish it?

The letter, and so the error contained in it (if it was an error), it was private, and so private that I know no man that has a copy of it, no not [even] myself who penned it (for aught I could find), but himself only. If I did offend him by writing of such an error to him (though by himself entreated to express my judgment), let him remember he pleaded for liberty of conscience. I wrote my conscience and the truth of God according to my conscience in the sight of God. Why should he punish me with open penance, and expose me (as much as in him lies, before the world) to open shame, as a man of blood, for the liberty of my conscience? How will it stand with his own principles to plead for liberty of conscience and yet to punish it? Besides, let him remember if I did offend him with such an error, it was but a private offense, and the rule of the Gospel required he should first have convinced and admonished me privately of it, and so have proceeded upon

John Cotton, *The Bloudy Tenent, Washed, And made White in the bloud of the Lambe: being discussed and discharged of bloud-guiltiness by just Defence.* . . . (London, 1647), pp. 1-2.

my contumacy, at length, to have told the church before he published it to the world. But such as seek for new Apostles must seek also for new Gospel before this manner of dealing can be justified by the Gospel of Christ. That book of his, therefore, being thus begun against the rule of the Gospel, no marvel if it swerve from the truth of the Gospel all along. He that sets forth out of his way in the first entrance of his journey, no marvel if he wander all the day after. . . .

A Reply to Mr. Williams

John Cotton

Such a letter to such a purpose I do remember I wrote unto Mr. Williams about half-a-score years ago. But whether this printed letter be a true copy thereof, or no, I do not know; for the letter being sent so long since, and no copy of it (that I can find) reserved by me, I can own it no further than I find the matter and style expressing the judgment which I then had of his cause of separation [banishment] and the affection which I bore unto his person. And for ought I see, the letter does not unfitly express both.

But how it came to be put in print I cannot imagine. Sure I am it was without my privity. And when I heard of it, it was unwelcome news . . . . There be [those] who think it was published by Mr. Williams himself, or by some of his friends who had the copy from him. Which latter might be the more probable, because himself denies the publishing of it. . . .

And in the Bay, not long before my coming, he began to oppose the King's patent with much vehemency (as he had done at Plymouth before), which made the magistrates to fear they should have more to do with him, than with a man publicly acknowledged to be godly and dearly beloved.

Soon after, when upon hearing of some Episcopal and malignant practices against the country, the magistrates and the whole General Court thought meet to take a trial of the fidelity of the people (not by imposing upon them, but) by offering to them an oath of fidelity; that in case any should refuse, they might not betrust them with [any] place of public command. He vehemently withstood it, partly

John Cotton, *A Reply to Mr. Williams His Examination* (1647), *The Writings of Roger Williams*, II, 9, 13-14, 18-20, 24, 41-51, 64.

because it was Christ's prerogative to have his office established by oath; partly, because an oath was a part of God's worship, and many of the people, being carnal (as he conceived it), it was not meet to put upon them an oath which was a part of God's worship. Upon such and the like disturbances to the civil peace (for upon this sundry refused the oath, and upon their refusal the magistrates could not discern how the people stood affected to the public safety), therefore, both the magistrates and sundry elders (though I do not remember myself to be one), advised the church of Salem not to proceed to choose him (as they were about then to do) unto office [of teacher] in the church. Yea, and in Salem (though many of the members were taken with him), some judicious among them told me they could not choose him to office, because they found him to be (contrary to the Apostle's rule) . . . self-pleasing, self-full, or as it is translated, self-willed. Nevertheless, the major part of the church made the choice of him. Soon after the church of Salem made suit to the [General] Court for a parcel of land which lay commodious for them. But the church delayed to hearken to their motion in forbearing the choice of Mr. Williams. Which so incensed Mr. Williams, that he caused the church to join with him in writing letters of admonition to all the churches whereof any of the magistrates were members, to admonish their magistrates of their breach of the rule of justice, in not granting their petition. Which following upon all the former disturbances raised by Mr. Williams, it still aggravated the former jealousies which, generally, the judicious sort of Christians had conceived of his self-conceited, and unquiet, and unlamblike frame of his spirit. . . .

"But whereas," he says, "he was exposed to the mercies of an howling wilderness in frost and snow, etc."

The truth is, the sentence of his banishment out of the patent was pronounced against him in the [General] Court before winter; and respite was given to him to tarry certain weeks (six or more) to prepare for his journey.

In the meantime, some of his friends went to the place appointed by himself beforehand, to make provision of housing and other necessaries for him against his coming. Otherwise, he might have chosen to have gone either southward to his acquaintances at Plymouth, or eastward to Pascatogue or Aganimticus. And then the wilderness had been as no wilderness (at least, no howling wilderness), where men sit down under warm and dry roofs, sheltered from the annoyance of frost and snow, and other winter hardships.

When he says, "That myself professed in speech and writing that I was no procurer of his sorrows," I do not believe that I made any such profession at all, either in speech or writing. For it was my serious intendment . . . to have procured his unfeigned godly sorrow for his errors in judgment, and for his offensive disturbances of churches and commonwealth. But this is that which I have professed, that I had no hand in procuring, or soliciting, the sentence of his banishment. And that not for the cause . . . as if I had some reluctancy in myself, concerning the way of persecution.

For, 1. I never did doubt that the way of persecution, (truly so called) that is, the affliction of others for righteousness' sake, was utterly unlawful.

2. I did never believe that the sentence passed against him was an act of persecution.

3. Nor did I ever see cause to doubt, but that in some causes (such as this of his was), banishment is a lawful and just punishment —if it be in proper speech a punishment at all in such a country as this is, where the jurisdiction (whence a man is banished) is but small, and the country round about it large and fruitful; where a man may make his choice of variety of more pleasant and profitable seats than he leaves behind him. In which respect, banishment in this country is not counted so much a confinement, as an enlargement, where a man does not so much lose civil comforts, as change them. And as for spiritual liberties (liberty of church ordinances), they were a burden and bondage to his spirit here [in Massachusetts]. And, therefore, he cast them off before they left him. . . .

But as for the true cause why I meddled not in his civil censure, it was chiefly because civil censures belong unto another kingdom than that which we [clergymen] are called to administer. (Civil censures are not the weapons of our warfare.) And partly also because I was carried (as still I am) with a compassion of his person, and likewise of his wife . . . .

I bless the Lord I am not ignorant that love covers a multitude of offenses; and that the disciples of Christ, when they are reviled, are taught to bless. And, therefore, were the case merely my own, and all the reproaches and slanders cast upon myself, had terminated in myself, I should have been as a deaf man, and as a dumb man that opens not his lips. But when, through my sides, not only so many elders and churches in this country, who had as much (or more) influence into his sufferings as myself, . . . yea, when court of justice suffer for justice's sake; yea, further, when the truth and righteousness of God also suffer for inflicting just recompense of reward upon the disturbers of civil and sacred truth and peace, and under pretence of maintaining liberty of conscience, purity of conscience is violated and destroyed. In such a case as this, just it is, and equal, rather that the name of an evil worker should justly suffer, than that the name of God, called upon judgment's seat, upon the Churches of Christ, and upon the ministers of the Gospel, should unjustly suffer for his sake. . . .

It was not my intent in that letter which he examines to discuss the grounds of his civil banishment at all; neither did I discuss one or another of them. And it is a preposterous shifting of the state of the question to put it upon me to give account of the causes of his banishment, who neither did banish him nor provoked the [General] Court to banish him out of the country. The magistrates and deputies of the commonwealth (who were then the members of that [General] Court) are all of them of age, and able themselves to give account of their own actions. To them, or some of them, he should in reason have addressed himself for satisfaction in this case (if any were due) and not to me . . . .

Whom that eminent magistrate was that so summed up the grounds of Mr. Williams his banishment in those four particulars above mentioned, Mr. Williams does wisely conceal his name, lest if he were named, he should be occasioned to bear witness against such fraudulent expression of the particulars. Whereof, some were no causes of his banishment at all, and such as were causes, were not delivered in such general terms. . . . It is evident the two latter causes which he gives of his banishment were no causes at all, as he expresses them. There are many known to hold both these opinions: "That it is not lawful to hear any of the ministers of the parish assemblies in England"; and "that the civil magistrate's power extends only to the bodies and goods and outward estates of men." And yet they are tolerated, not only to live in the commonwealth, but also in the fellowship of the churches.

The two former [reasons that Williams gives for his banishment], though they be not so much noised, yet there be many, if not most, that hold: "That we have not our land merely by right of patent from the King, but that the natives are true owners of all that they possess or improve." Neither do I know any among us that, either then were or now are, of another mind.

And as for the other point, "That it is not lawful to call a wicked person to swear or pray," though that be not commonly held, yet it is known to be held of some, who are tolerated to enjoy both civil and church liberties among us.

To come, therefore, to particulars: Two things there were which (to my best observation and remembrance) caused the sentence of his banishment; and two others fell in that hastened it.

1. His violent and tumultuous carriage against the patent.

By the patent it is that we received allowance from the King to depart his kingdom, and to carry our goods with us, without offense to his officers and without paying custom to himself.

By the patent certain select men (as magistrates and freemen) have power to make laws and the magistrates to execute justice and judgment among the people, according to such laws.

By the patent we have power to erect such a government of the church as is most agreeable to the Word, to the estate of the people, and to the gaining of natives (in God's time), first to civility, and then to Christianity.

To this authority established by this patent Englishmen do readily submit themselves; and foreign plantations (the French, the Dutch, and Swedish) do willingly transact their negotiations with us, as with a colony established by the royal authority of the state of England.

This patent Mr. Williams, publicly and vehemently, preached against, as containing matter of falsehood and injustice: Falsehood, in making the King the first Christian Prince who had discovered these parts; and injustice in giving the country to his English subjects, which belonged to the native Indians. This, therefore, he pressed upon the magistrates and the people, to be humbled for from time to time in days of solemn humiliation, and to return the patent back again to the King. It was answered to him, first, that it was neither the King's intendment, nor the English planters', to take possession of the country by murder of the natives or by robbery. But either to take possession of the void places of the country by the law of nature (for *vacuum domicilium credit occupanti*), or if we took any lands from the natives, it was by way of purchase and free consent. . . .

This answer did not satisfy Mr. Williams, who pleaded, the natives, though they did not nor could not subdue the country . . . , yet they hunted all the country over . . . and, therefore, as noble men in England possessed great parks, and the King great forests in England, only for their game, and no man might lawfully invade their propriety, so might the natives challenge the like propriety of the country here. . . .

But these answers not satisfying him, this was still pressed by him as a national sin to hold the patent, yea, and a national duty to renounce the patent, which to have done, would have subverted the fundamental state and government of the country.

2. The second offense which procured his banishment was occasioned [by the problem of the oath], as I touched before. The magistrates and other members of the General Court, upon intelligence of some Episcopal and malignant practices against the country, they made an order of [the General] Court to take trial of the fidelity of the people (not by imposing upon them, but) by offering to them an oath of fidelity; that in case any should refuse to take it, they might not betrust them with place of public charge and command. This oath, when it came abroad, he vehemently withstood it and dissuaded sundry from it. . . . So the [General] Court was forced to desist from that proceeding. Which practice of his was held to be the more dangerous, because it tended to unsettle all the kingdoms and commonwealths in Europe.

These were (as I took it) the causes of his banishment. Two other things fell in upon these that hastened the sentence. The former fell out thus: The magistrates discerning by the former passages, the heady and turbulent spirit of Mr. Williams, both they and others advised the church of Salem not to call him to office in their church; nevertheless, the major part of the church made choice of him. Soon after, when the church made suit to the [General] Court for a parcel of land adjoining to them, the [General] Court delayed to grant their request (as has been mentioned before) because the church had refused to hearken to the magistrates and others in forbearing the choice of Mr. Williams. Whereupon, Mr. Williams took occasion to stir up the church to join with him in writing letters of admonition unto all the churches whereof those magistrates were members, to admonish them of their open transgression of the rule of justice. Which letters coming to the several churches, provoked the magistrates to take the more speedy course with so heady and violent a spirit.

But to prevent his sufferings (if it might be), it was moved by some of the elders that themselves might have liberty (according to the rule of Christ) to deal with him, and with the church also in a church-way. It might be, the church might hear us, and he the church. Which, being consented to, some of our churches wrote to the church of Salem, to present before them the offensive spirit and way of their officer (Mr. Williams), both in judgment and practice. The church finally began to hearken to us, and, accordingly, began to address themselves to the healing of his spirit. Which he discerning, renounced communion with the church of Salem, pretending they held communion with the churches in the Bay, and the churches in the Bay held communion with the parish churches in England . . . . But this carriage of his in renouncing the church upon such an occasion, and with them all the churches in the country, and the spreading of his leaven to sundry that resorted to him, this gave the magistrates the more cause to observe the heady unruliness of his spirit and the incorrigibleness thereof by any church-way, all the churches in the country being then renounced by him. And this was the other occasion which hastened the sentence of his banishment, upon the former grounds. . . .

Whereupon, the magistrates being to assemble to the next General Court at Newtown, intending (as appeared by the event) to proceed against him. And one of the magistrates of our town [Boston], being to go thither, acquainted me that it was likely Mr. Williams his cause would then be issued, and asked me what I thought of it. "Truly," said I, "I pity the man, and have already interceded for him, while there was any hope of doing good. But now, he having refused to hear both his own church, and us, and having rejected us all, as no churches of Christ before any conviction, we have now no more to say in his behalf, nor hope to prevail for him. We have told the governor and magistrates before, that if our labor [to change his opinions] was in vain, we could not help it but must sit down. And you know they are generally so much incensed against his course that it is not your voice, nor the voices of two or three more, that can suspend the sentence." Some further speech I had with him of my own marvel at the weakness and slenderness of the grounds of his opinions, notions, and courses, and yet carried on with such vehemency and impetuousness and precedence of spirit. . . .

part two

ROGER WILLIAMS,
JOHN COTTON,
AND THE PROBLEMS
OF CHURCH AND STATE

Roger Williams returned to England in 1643 with a powerful sense of mission. He was determined to advocate his own resolution of the dangerous crisis concerning church and state. Williams' publications aroused the Massachusetts Bay Colony and called forth the rebuttal of John Cotton. The eminent Cotton engaged Williams in this great debate with considerable regret and embarrassment. Their clash of principles caught the attention of public opinion during a turbulent period of history.

The documents that follow illustrate different aspects of the conflict between Williams and Cotton. Among the issues on which they differed, those of the nature of religious liberty, the role of government, and the relevance of Scripture, theology, history, and peace to the relationship of church and state, have been selected as representative of their controversy. Sources also have been chosen to show the impact of the ideas of Williams and Cotton on the arguments among English writers.

Another group of sources has been assembled to record the way Williams and Cotton applied their principles in Massachusetts and Rhode Island. Both men occupy an interesting place in the intellectual history of the western world, because each had an opportunity to put into practice the ideas he expounded in the transatlantic debate. Led by Cotton and other ministers, Massachusetts set up a uniform system of worship and penalized those who dissented from the establishment. Rhode Island offered a sanctuary for every religious persuasion in the seventeenth century. Periodically, adherents of proscribed dominations infiltrated into Massachusetts from Rhode Island and carried on religious services in contempt of the law. These incursions were met with corporal punishment and fines, which were imposed to ward off further onslaughts by religious dissenters. The final sources concern the dramatic encounter between three Baptists, led by Dr. John Clarke, a Rhode Island physician, and the Massachusetts government. This struggle raised charges of religious persecution and prompted an indirect exchange of views between Roger Williams and John Cotton.

Government and Religious Freedom

Roger Williams

Truth. . . . no man denies a double ministry.

The one appointed by Christ Jesus in His Church, to gather, to govern, receive in, cast out, and order all the affairs of the Church, the House, City or Kingdom of God.

Secondly, a civil ministry, or office merely human and civil, which men agree to constitute, called therefore an human creation, and is as true and lawful in those nations, cities, kingdoms, etc., which never heard of the true God, nor His holy Son, Jesus, as in any part of the world besides, where the name of Jesus is most taken up.

From all which premises, viz., that the scope of the spirit of God . . . is to handle the matters of the second table [of the Ten Commandments] . . . since the magistrates, of whom Paul wrote, were natural, ungodly, persecuting, and yet lawful magistrates, and to be obeyed in all lawful civil things.

Since all magistrates are God's ministers, essentially civil, bounded to a civil work, with civil weapons or instruments, and paid or rewarded with civil rewards. From all which, I say, . . . [it] cannot truly be alleged by any for the power of the civil magistrate to be exercised in spiritual and soul matters. . . .

Peace. Some will here ask: what may the magistrate then lawfully do . . . in matters of religion? . . .

Truth. The civil magistrate either respects that religion and worship which his conscience is persuaded is true, and upon which he ventures his soul, or else that and those which he is persuaded are false.

Roger Williams, *The Bloudy Tenent, of Persecution, for cause of Conscience, discussed, in A Conference between Truth and Peace* (1644), *The Writings of Roger Williams*, III, 161-62, 372-73, 398-99.

Concerning the first, if that which the magistrate believes to be true, be true, I say he owes a three-fold duty unto it:

First, approbation and countenance, a reverent esteem and honorable testimony . . . with a tender respect of truth and the professors of it.

Secondly, personal submission of his own soul to the power of the Lord Jesus, in that spiritual government and kingdom. . . .

Thirdly, protection of such true professors of Christ, whether apart, or meeting together, as also of their estates from violence and injury . . . .

Now, secondly, if it be a false religion (unto which the civil magistrate dare not join, yet), he owes:

First, permission (for approbation he owes not to what is evil), and this . . . for public peace and quiet sake.

Secondly, he owes protection to the persons of his subjects (though of a false worship), that no injury be offered either to the persons or goods of any. . . .

But (to wind up all) as it is most true that magistracy in general is of God for the preservation of mankind in civil order and peace (the world, otherwise, would be like the sea, wherein men, like fishes, would hunt and devour each other and the greater devour the lesser), so also it is true, that magistracy . . . is of man. Now what kind of magistrate soever the people shall agree to set up, whether he receive Christianity before he be set in office, or whether he receive Christianity after, he receives no more power of magistracy than a magistrate that has received no Christianity. For neither of them both can receive more than the commonweal, the body of people and civil state, as men, communicate unto them and betrust them with.

All lawful magistrates in the world . . . have, and can have no more power, than fundamentally lies in the bodies of fountains themselves, which power, might, or authority, is not religious, Christian, etc., but natural, human, and civil.

And hence, it is true, that a Christian captain, Christian merchant, physician, lawyer, pilot, father, master, and (so, consequently,) magistrate, etc., is no more a captain, merchant, physician, lawyer, pilot, father, master, magistrate, etc., than a captain, merchant, etc., of any other conscience or religion. . . .

A pagan or anti-Christian pilot may be as skillful to carry the ship to its desired port as any Christian mariner or pilot in the world, and may perform that work with as much safety and speed. . . .

Limits of the Civil Magistrate

Roger Williams

1. That in these late years God has made it evident that all civil magistracy in the world is merely and essentially civil. And that the civil magistrate can truly take cognizance of nothing as a civil magistrate but what is proper and within his civil sphere. The magistrate, if a saint, has a spiritual power, and so have all saints; and he that partakes more of Christ's spirit, has more of Christ's power, whatever his outward condition be.

2. By the last will and testament of Christ Jesus, we find not the least title of commission to the civil magistrate (as civil) to judge and act in the matters of His spiritual kingdom. . . .

Hence, although it be the duty of Kings, Queens, magistrates, to be nursing fathers and mothers to the saints; although it be the saints' duty to pray for magistrates, that they may live peaceably under them in all godliness and honesty; yet, suppose the magistrates be never so ungodly, idolatrous, blasphemous, bloody (as they were in the first 300 years after Christ), yet Christ Jesus failed not, nor will, to preserve his saints in the power and spirit of true Christianity and godliness. . . .

The Parliament established King Henry VIII Head of the Church [of England]. This supremacy has continued in four Protestant Princes since. Yet, first, what disagreements about the title? For while the clergy have preached . . . the Prince's authority in spirituals, after the pattern of the Kings of Israel and Judah, the truth is, that Parliaments,

Roger Williams, *The Fourth Paper, Presented by Major Butler, To the Honourable Committee of Parliament* (1652), *The Complete Writings of Roger Williams*, 7 vols. (New York: Russell & Russell, Inc., Publishers, 1963), VII, 133-37. Reprinted by kind permission.

and people, since have pleaded, that Princes could not receive but what the Parliaments gave them, and the Parliaments could not give them but what the people gave the Parliaments, their representative; which could not possibly be a spiritual and soul power.

Secondly, the work [of a church-state union] has never prospered. . . .

My humble prayer shall be to Him that is only wise, so to guide this renowned Parliament that they may see and shun the rocks on which our fathers (as touching a state religion), both Papist and Protestant, have made most woeful shipwreck. And that they may be pleased to remember . . . the Lord Jesus will sooner or later eradicate and pluck them up, until at last the work and glory be given to Him-self, to work freely and in His own way, by the free breathings of His most powerful spirit in the mouths and hearts of such by whom, and in whom, He freely pleases.

Hence, oh that it would please the Father of Spirits, to affect the heart of the Parliament with such a merciful sense of the soul-bars and yokes which our fathers have laid upon the neck of this nation, and at last to proclaim a true and absolute soul freedom to all the people of the land impartially; so that no person be forced to pray, nor pay, otherwise than as his soul believes and consents. . . .

I humbly conceive it to be the duty of the civil magistrate to break down that superstitious wall of separation (as to civil things) between us Gentiles and the Jews, and freely (without their asking) to make way for their free and peaceable habitation among us. And the rather because that people (however for a season under a most terrible eclipse) yet,

1. The Holy Scripture says that they are a beloved people, and beloved (as we sometimes love unworthy children) for their Father's sake.

2. They are a people, above all the peoples and nations in the world, under the most gracious and express promises.

3. We Gentiles by their fall have had the occasion of our rising to the blessed and joyful knowledge of a Saviour.

4. Their rising again to own and embrace Christ Jesus is promised to be as life from the dead, not only to themselves, but as to the propagating of Christ Jesus to other people.

5. Out of some kind of sense of these things, we pretend to look and long and pray for their return and calling.

6. As other nations, so this especially, and the Kings thereof,

have had just cause to fear, that the unchristian oppressions, incivilities, and inhumanities of this nation against the Jews have cried to heaven against this nation and the Kings and Princes of it.

What horrible oppressions and horrible slaughters have the Jews suffered from the Kings and peoples of this nation in the reigns of Henry II, King John, Richard I, and Edward I. . . .

Duties of the Civil Magistrate

Roger Williams

What is, then, the express duty of the civil magistrate as to Christ Jesus, His Gospel, and kingdom? . . .

First, in removing the civil bars, obstructions, hindrances, in taking off those yokes that pinch the very souls and consciences of men, such as yet are the payments of tithes and the maintenance of ministers they have no faith in; such are the enforced oaths, and some ceremonies therein, in all the Courts of Justice; such are the holy martyrings, holy buryings, etc.

Secondly, in a free and absolute permission of the consciences of all men, in what is merely spiritual, not the very consciences of the Jews, nor the consciences of the Turks or Papists, or pagans themselves excepted.

But how will this propagate the Gospel of Christ Jesus?

I answer thus: The first grand design of Christ Jesus is to destroy and consume His mortal enemy, Antichrist. This must be done by the breath of His mouth in His prophets and witnesses. Now the nations of the world have impiously stopped this heavenly breath, and stifled the Lord Jesus in His servants. . . .

Roger Williams, *The Hireling Ministry None of Christs, or A Discourse touching the Propagating of the Gospel of Christ Jesus* (1652), *The Complete Writings of Roger Williams*, VII, 178-79. Reprinted by kind permission.

source 8

New England's Persecution

Roger Williams

My end is to discover and proclaim the crying and horrible guilt of the bloody doctrine [of persecution] as one of the most seditious, destructive, blasphemous, and bloodiest in any or all the nations of the world, notwithstanding the many fine veils, pretenses and colors of not persecuting Christ Jesus, but heretics, not God's truth or servants, but blasphemers, seducers; not persecuting men for their conscience, but for sinning against their conscience, etc.

My end is to persuade God's Judah (especially) to wash their hands from blood, to cleanse their hearts and ways from such unchristian practices toward all that is man, capable of a religion and a conscience, but most of all toward Christ Jesus, who cries out (as He did to Saul) in the sufferings of the least of His servants: Old England, Old England, New England, New England, King, King, Parliaments, Parliaments, General Courts, General Courts, Presbyterians, Presbyterians, Independents, Independents, etc., why persecute you me? . . .

Truth. I desire my rejoinder may be as full of love as truth; yet some say Master Cotton is wise, and knows in what door the wind blows of late. He is not ignorant of what sad complaints in letters, printings, conferences, so many of God's people (and of his own conscience and judgment of Independency) have poured forth against New England's persecuting, etc. He knows what bars New England's bloody

Roger Williams, *The Bloody Tenent yet More Bloody: by Mr. Cottons endeavour to wash it white in the Blood of the Lambe* (1652), *The Writings of Roger Williams* (Providence, R.I.: Narragansett Club Publications, 1866-1874), IV, 26, 51, 395-96.

tenet and practice may put to his brethren's just desires and suits for moderation and toleration to non-conforming consciences. . . .

Notwithstanding Mr. Cotton's cloak, to wit, that they will not meddle with the heretic before he has sinned against his own conscience, and so persecute him only for sinning against his own conscience, yet I earnestly beseech every reader seriously to ponder the whole stream and series of Mr. Cotton's discourse, propositions, affirmations, etc., through the whole book [*The Bloudy Tenent, Washed*], and he shall then be able to judge whether it be untrue that his doctrine tends not to constrain nor restrain conscience.

2. For the matter of fact, how can he with any humility before the flaming eyes of the Most High cry out no such practice, when:

First, their laws cry out a command under penalty for all to come to church though not to be members, which, in truth, . . . is but a color and vizard deceiving himself and others. And a cruel law is yet extant . . . against Anabaptistry, etc.

Secondly, their practice cries their imprisonments, finings, whippings, banishments, cry in the ears of the Lord of Hosts, and the louder because of such unchristian figleaves, cloaks, etc. . . .

God's Unchangeable Law for Dissenters

John Cotton

That upon the discovery of the deadly corruption of the [Catholic] religion of the See of Rome, it was a righteous judgment of God, and such as argued Him, unchangeable ever like Himself, that the priests and Jesuits who carried that religion up and down the nations should be adjudged or condemned to a bloody death. . . .

We opened and showed before . . . that both their doctrine and worship and government was deadly, and such as was utterly unwholesome, both for private families and states, church and commonwealths; and so corrupt, as was deadly; whoever lived and died in that religion, lived an hypocrite and died a reprobate. Now the next Angel that comes upon this discovery, he "pours his vial on the rivers and fountains of water, and they become blood (Rev. 16:4)." That is, they make laws to adjudge all that carry that religion up and down the nation to be guilty of blood, and, therefore, to be put to death as traitors and rebels against the state. And this is acknowledged by the Angels of God, I mean those that are ministers of God's justice, and approve this testimony as authentic; they acknowledge this a righteous judgment of God, as He that is, was, and shall always be one and the same. Thus He was wont to carry it, and thus He does still. In old time, if a man played the false prophet, and suggested such devices as these [i.e., Roman Catholicism], the Lord judged him to death; this was His manner. And so in the New Testament as in the Old, He condemns all such to death, and He is most righteous in so doing. This is the sum.

John Cotton, *The Powring out of the Seven Vials: or an Exposition of the 16. Chapter of the Revelation, with an Application of it to our Times* (London: 1642), Part 3, pp. 8-12, 14-15.

It was a great while before this, though not full two thousand years, when Zachary prophesied that "God would cut off the false prophet," in the Zach. 13:2-3, "and if there were any false prophet should arise, his father and mother should thrust him through, because he spoke lies in the name of the God of truth, he should not live." And they speak not of his typical death, that is, of his death by church censure or banishment, which have a kind of death in them; but they speak of such a death as that he was not worthy to live—to cast a lie upon the God of Truth, the Oracle of Truth. But long before Zachary this was an ancient law of Moses in the Deuteronomy 13. This was a law that false prophets, they that turned religion to the blood of a dead man, that did fundamentally pervert religion, they should not live. And mind the reason that God gives here, partly in this text, and partly in other Scriptures.

It is taken from the heinousness of blasphemy in the Leviticus 24: 16: "He that blasphemes the name of God, shall surely be put to death." Every blasphemer shall be put to death. Now we cannot excuse Popish priests and Jesuits from gross blasphemy. . . .

As all blasphemous heretics, so seducing heretics are to be put to death. . . . Therefore, by the ancient laws of that unchangeable God that thought it insufferable in those days, He thinks it insufferable now that priests and Jesuits should bring in other altars, other mediations and mediators, as prayers of saints and angels; the Lord looks at it as deeply meritorious of a bloody death, as in former times. He is the same God, and His zeal and jealousy is deeply provoked against the like kind of viciousness now as it ever was then. . . .

The fourth reason [for the prosecution of priests and Jesuits] is taken from that which the *Justitia Britanniae* stands most upon, and becomes statesmen to do; and that is the conspiracy and treason against the state. And that unavoidably, by suffering such locust to run up and down the country, to poison the hearts of men by their corrupt ways and means; for these ministers, they do unavoidably, not accidently, but they unavoidably, draw men from their allegiance due to their native Prince to a foreign state. For if a Prince should profess Protestant religion (which is the true religion), and thereupon be excommunicated by the Bishop of Rome, what then? . . .

And for a fifth reason, . . . from the law of retaliation, that looks how men have dealt with others, they should be so dealt with themselves. Now these priests and Jesuits, and their abettors, in the time of Queen Mary and Henry VIII . . . if a man were suspected of heretical depravity, and pronounced guilty thereof by the [Catholic] Church, he was to be delivered to the secular power, only he might have leave to consider of it. But if he fell again, there was no hope of mercy, but he must look for blood, as if he were no better than a child of death. And yet they were men that never troubled the state, but quietly suffered for their religion and conscience. So that these Jesuits and priests, delivering up so many innocent lambs of Christ, ministers of the Gospel and holy saints, to the secular power, to be burned at the stake. . . . Therefore, look as they have measured to others, it is measured to them, by the ancient law of God . . . . So you see this point is plain . . . that the priests and Jesuits which carried . . . that religion up and down the nation should be condemned to a bloody death; you see the truth of the point, and the reasons of it. . . .

It has been a just hand of God, that they that worry (like ravenous wolves) the souls of God's people, should themselves be worried; that they that have made firebrands of [Protestant] Christians should drink blood themselves; they that overwhelmed Christians in confusion and tumult, it is just with God that they should be overwhelmed; they that have been so busy in putting to death innocents, that they should also be put to death. You see this is just with God, it is well becoming to the unchangeable righteousness of God. Thus it was in the Old Testament, and why should it be changed in the New? . . .

source 10

Massachusetts Does Not Persecute

John Cotton

In printing my answer to the prisoner's letter [about religious persecution], he [Williams] prefixed this title: "The answer of Mr. John Cotton of Boston in New England professedly maintaining Persecution for cause of Conscience."

This title trespasses not only against the Creator of Christian love, which is wont to take even doubtful things in the fairest sense; but even against the law of truth. For in the whole purport of my answer to the letter, both in stating the question and in answering objections, I expressly profess: 1. That no man is to be persecuted at all (much less for conscience sake), because all persecution is oppression for righteousness sake. 2. I profess further, that none is to be punished for his conscience sake, though erroneous, unless his errors be fundamental, or seditiously and turbulently promoted, and that after due conviction of conscience. That it may appear, he is not punished for his conscience, but for sinning against his conscience.

Thus while he pleads for liberty of conscience, he takes liberty to his conscience openly to publish that I do professedly maintain persecution for cause of conscience, when I do in express terms professedly renounce it. This liberty of conscience sets the conscience at liberty . . . .

In points of doctrine (I said in my answer to the prisoner's letter), "some are fundamental, without right belief, whereof a man cannot be saved; others are circumstantial and less principal, wherein one man may differ from another in judgment without prejudice of salvation on either part. . . ."

John Cotton, *The Bloudy Tenent, Washed* (1647), pp. 2-3, 5, 9-10, 20-21, 27, 35, 67-68, 112-13, 147-49, 165.

Fundamental doctrines are of two sorts. Some hold forth the foundation of Christian religion, as the doctrines of salvation by Christ and of faith in His name, repentance from dead works, resurrection from the dead, and the like. Others concern the foundation of the church, as the matter and form of it, and the proper adjuncts accompanying the same. . . .

I speak of the former sort of these only, namely, the foundation or fundamental points of Christian religion, which who so subverts and renounces, he renounces also his own salvation. The other sort I look at as less principal in comparison of these, though some of them have a fundamental use in church order. . . .

That fundamentals are so clear, that a man cannot but be convinced in conscience of the truth of them after two or three admonitions; and that, therefore, such a person as still continues obstinate is condemned of himself. And if he then be punished, he is not punished for his conscience, but for sinning against his own conscience. . . .

Though I do maintain (as the Apostle does) a clearness of fundamental points of religion and worship (such fundamentals, I say, without which fellowship with God cannot be had), and though I grant, that in subverting such fundamental points and persisting therein after once or twice admonition, a man sins against his own conscience and is, therefore, censurable by the church, yea and by the civil magistrate also, if, after conviction, he continue to seduce others unto his damnable heresy, yet I do not herein measure to others that which myself, when I lived in such practices, would not have assured to myself.

For I thank God, God never left me to live in any such practices as to fall into any fundamental error, much less to persist therein after conviction and admonition, and least of all to seduce others thereinto. If God should leave me so far as to fall so fearfully into this three-fold degree of heretical wickedness, what am I better than other men? Better myself cut off by death or banishment, than the flock of Christ to be seduced and destroyed by my heretical wickedness. . . .

God in times past suffered all nations to walk in their own ways. And so did His viceregents, the good Kings of Israel, do the like. David did not compel the tributary nations to worship the God of Israel. No more does our colony here compel the tributary Indians to worship our God. But if an Israelite forsakes God, he disturbs not only the Commonwealth of Israel, but the barks of pagans and heathen states, as Jonah did this ship by his departure from God. Therefore, a Christian by departing from God may disturb a gentile civil state. And it is no pre-

posterous way for the governors of the state, according to the quality
of the disturbance raised by the starting aside of such a Christian, to
punish both it and him by civil censure.

Nor does the civil state in such punishments attend . . . to procure the conversion of heretics, or apostates, or such like scandalous,
turbulent offenders, as how to prevent the perversion of their sounder
people . . . or else, to work the subversion of such as do subvert both
truth and peace. . . .

Nor is the righteous proceeding in civil states a disquieting of
themselves, or any unmerciful disquieting of others. For it is no disquieting to a just man to do justice; and the disquieting of men in sin,
it is no unmerciful dealing, but a compassionate healing, either of
themselves or others. The false prophet reclaimed by stigmatizing with
wounds in his hands will freely acknowledge: "Thus I was wounded in
the house of my friends. Friends are not unmerciful disquieters. . . ."

But it was no part of my words or meaning to say that every heretic,
though erring in some fundamental and weighty points, and for the
same excommunicated [by the church], shall forthwith be punished by
the civil magistrate; unless it does afterwards appear, that he break
forth further either into blasphemy, or idolatry, or seducement of others
to his heretical, pernicious ways. . . .

I would not say that every man that holds forth error in a boisterous and arrogant spirit to the disturbance of civil peace ought to
be punished with death. This is too bloody a tenet, unless the boisterous arrogancy were such as did disturb the civil peace to the destruction
of the lives and souls of men. . . .

Discusser [Roger Williams]

But the civil magistrate has his charge of the bodies and goods of
the subject; as the spiritual officers of Christ's city or kingdom have
the charge of their souls and soul-safety.

Defender [John Cotton]

Reply 1. If it were true, that the magistrate has charge only of
the bodies and goods of the subject, yet that might justly excite to watch-
fulness against such pollutions of religion as tend to apostasy. For if
the church and people of God fall away from God, God will visit the

city and country with public calamity, if not captivity, for the church's sake. . . .

Reply 2. It is a carnal and wordly and, indeed, an ungodly imagination to confine the magistrate's charge to the bodies and goods of the subject, and to exclude them from the care of their souls. Did ever God commit the charge of the body to any governors to whom he did not commit (in His way) the care of souls also? Has God committed to parents the charge of the children's bodies, and not the care of their souls? To masters the charge of their servants' bodies, and not of their souls? To captains the charge of their soldiers' bodies, and not of their souls? Shall the captains suffer false worship, yea idolatry, publicly professed and practiced in the camp, and yet look to prosper in battle? The magistrates, to whom God has committed the charges of bodies and outward man of the subject, are they not also to take care to procure faithful teachers to be sent among them? . . . The truth is, church governors and civil governors do herein stand parallel one to another. The church governors, though to them be chiefly committed the charge of souls as their adequate objects, yet, in order to the good of the souls of their people, to exhort from idleness, negligence, from intemperancy in meats and drinks, from oppression, and deceit, and therein provide both for the health of their bodies and the safety of their estates. So civil governors, though to them be chiefly committed the bodies and goods of the people (as their adequate object), yet, in order to [accomplish] this, they may, and ought to, procure spiritual helps to their souls and to prevent such spiritual evils as that the prosperity of religion among them might advance the prosperity of the civil state. . . .

. . . I willingly grant it may be lawful for a civil magistrate to tolerate notorious evil doers in two cases under which all the examples will fall which the Discusser [Williams] alleges in any word of truth.

As first, in regard of the efficient cause of punishing. When the magistrate's hand is too weak and feeble, and the offender's adherents so great and strong that justice cannot be done upon him without manifest peril to the whole state, there the magistrate may tolerate a notorious evil, even murder itself . . . .

And, secondly, in regard of the final cause, an evil may be tolerated to prevent other greater evils—as Moses tolerated divorce of unpleasing wives to prevent the murder or other hard and cruel usage of them.

In either of these cases, I would not deny but a murderer may be tolerated: if either the magistrate wants sufficient power, with safety of the state to cut him off; or if a foreign state be so affected and addicted to the murderer, that in case the magistrate here cut off him, they will cut off sundry of our innocent and necessary members, whom they have gotten into their custody in revenge of him.

And if either of these be the case, I easily grant that it is not evil to tolerate a notorious, seducing false teacher, or other scandalous liver. But such an extraordinary does not hinder the due largesse and generality of the proposition that it is evil to tolerate seditious evil doers, seducing teachers, [and] scandalous livers. . . .

But to return to our Discusser [Williams], he speaks at random when he intimates that we walk "not by rule, but partially, as if we permitted not the like liberty of worship to our countrymen, nor to the French, Dutch, Spanish, Persians, Turks, Jews, which we do to the Indians."

For we neither constrain them to worship God with us, nor restrain them from worshipping God in their own way. Persians, Turks and Jews come not among us; those of other nations of Europe, when they do come among us, their manner of worship is not taken notice of among us. Our countrymen worship God with us for the most part; if some of them come not to our assemblies by reason of the distance of their dwellings from us, they have liberty of public prayer and preaching of the word among themselves, by such as themselves choose, without disturbance. . . .

Neither is it true that we suffer no man of any different conscience or worship to live in our jurisdiction. For not to speak of Presbyterians, who do not only live among us, but exercise their public ministry without disturbance, there be Anabaptists and Antinomians tolerated to live not only in our jurisdictions, but even in some of our churches. "Yea," said the Discusser [Williams], "but they must actually submit to come to our church."

I cannot say, nor do I believe, that any man is compelled to come into our church against his conscience. . . .

I cannot call to mind . . . any man in this country was ever compelled to hear the word of God in any of our churches in this country. . . .

The Beauty of Religious Constraint

John Cotton

It is no impeachment of church liberty, but an enlargement of its beauty and honor, to be bound by strict laws and holy commandments, to observe the pure worship of God, and to be subject unto due punishment for the gross violation of the same. . . .

It is a great advancement to the beauty and comeliness of a church [and] state, when people and magistrates do both consent together to purge the whole country, even to the utmost borders of the churches, from corruption in religion, and to adorn the same with exemplary justice upon notorious offenders . . . .

John Cotton, *A Brief Exposition With Practical Observations Upon the whole Book of Canticles Never Before Printed* (London: 1655), p. 26.

Heresy Is Not the Truth

John Cotton

If every anti-Christian doctrine be a lie, then they that are born of it are not born of the truth, and the doctors of it are liars, so that . . . it is a lying doctrine they hold, those that are the doctors and teachers of their church are liars; and take the body of the church, it is a bulk of lies, a company of liars, deceiving the world, and sporting themselves in their deceiving. . . .

If no heresy be of the truth, then certainly it will never be for the truth; no stream rises higher than the spring from whence it comes. If such doctrine comes not from the truth, it will never rise so high as the truth. Never look for true dealing from an heretic that lies against the Gospel, and against his own conscience; never believe any doctrine of theirs, for they aim at subverting. If they deal not truly with God, they will not deal truly with man. . . .

It may teach us there is no safe reconciliation with these doctrines; nay, no safe toleration, for no lie is of the truth. How can you reconcile night and day? light and darkness? There is as wide a difference between the truth and anti-Christian doctrines; therefore, there is no safe toleration of them, but one of them will be rooting out the other, either lies or the truth will be banished. . . .

John Cotton, *A Practical Commentary, or An Exposition with Observations, Reasons, and Uses upon the First Epistle General of John* (London: 1656), pp. 174-75.

Scripture and Liberty of Conscience

Roger Williams

Peace. It is said by some: "Why then did Paul himself appeal to Caesar, unless that Caesar . . . ought to have been a fit judge in such [religious] matters?" [Acts 25:10, Then, said Paul, I stand at Caesar's judgment seat, where I ought to be judged. . . .]

Truth. I answer, if Paul in this appeal to Caesar had referred and submitted, simply and properly, the cause of Christ, His ministry and ministration, to the Roman Emperor's tribunal, knowing him to be an idolatrous stranger from the true God, and a lion-like bloody persecutor of the Lord Jesus, the Lamb of God, I say, let it be considered whether or not he had committed these five evils:

The first against the dimmest light of reason in appealing to darkness to judge light, to unrighteousness to judge righteousness, the spiritually blind to judge and end the controversy concerning heavenly colors.

Secondly, against the cause of religion, which if condemned by every inferior idolator, must needs be condemned by the Caesars themselves, who . . . set up their state images or religions, commanding the world's uniformity of worship to them.

Thirdly, against the holy state and calling of the Christians themselves, who (by virtue of their subjection to Christ), even the least of them, are in spiritual things above the highest potentates or Emperors in the world, who continue in enmity against or in ignorant natural state without Christ Jesus. . . .

Fourthly, against his own calling, apostleship, or office of ministry,

Roger Williams, *The Bloudy Tenent, of Persecution, for cause of Conscience* (1644), pp. 157-59.

unto which Caesar himself and all potentates (in spiritual and soul matters) ought to have submitted. . . .

And, if so, how should Paul appeal in spiritual things to Caesar, or write to the Churches of Jesus to submit in Christian or spiritual matters?

Fifthly, if Paul had appealed to Caesar in spiritual respects, he greatly profaned the holy name of God in holy things, in so improper and vain a prostitution of spiritual things to carnal and natural judgments, which are not able to comprehend spiritual matters, which are alone spiritually discerned.

And yet, Caesar (as a civil, supreme magistrate) ought to defend Paul from civil violence and slanderous accusations about sedition, mutiny, civil disobedience, etc. And in that sense who doubts but God's people may appeal to the Roman Caesar, an Egyptian Pharaoh, a Philistine Abimelech, an Assyrian Nebuchadnezzar, the great Mogol, Prester John, the great Turk, or an Indian Sachem? . . .

source 14

Scripture Allows the Government to Judge

John Cotton

Paul's appeal to Caesar was about the wrongs done unto the Jews (Acts 25:10). The wrongs to them were not only civil, but church offenses, which Paul denied. "Neither against the law of the Jews," said he, "nor against the temple, nor against Caesar, have I offended any thing at all. . . ." These things were matters of religion, as well as civil offenses. To offend against the law of the Jews and against the temple were offenses against religion; to offend against Caesar was a civil offense. To be judged of these things, Paul declined the court at Jerusalem (as being unjustly prejudiced against him). But professing his own innocence and subjection to just judgment, he appealed to Caesar's judgment seat, wherein three or four things do evidently appear:

1. That a man may be such an offender in matters of religion (against the law of God, against the church, as well as in civil matters against Caesar) as to be worthy of death. . . .

2. That Paul, or any such like servant of Christ, if he should commit any such offense, he would not refuse judgment unto death.

3. That for the judgment of his person in these causes (whether ecclesiastical or civil), it is lawful in some cases to appeal to a civil, though a pagan, magistrate. In some cases, I say, as where both [of] these concur, to wit: 1. That church officers are maliciously prejudiced against a man, and inferior civil courts incline to them. 2. That a man be called in question among them in capital causes, which concern his life.

But a fourth thing which appears from Paul's appeal is this: that the civil magistrate, whether Christian or pagan, may, and ought to . . . be able to judge, though not of all questions, yet of capital offenses against religion, as well as against the civil state. . . .

John Cotton, *The Bloudy Tenent, Washed* (1647), pp. 58-59.

The Old Testament and Liberty of Conscience

Roger Williams

Truth. . . . I have often touched those Scriptures produced from the practice of the Kings of Israel and Judah. Yet, because so great a weight of this controversy lies upon this precedent of the Old Testament, from the duties of this nature enjoined to those Kings and governors and their practices, obeying or disobeying, accordingly commended or reproved, I shall . . . declare and demonstrate how weak and brittle this supposed pillar of marble is to bear up and sustain such a mighty burden and weight of so many high concernments as are laid upon it. In which I shall evidently prove that the state of Israel, as a national state made up of spiritual and civil power, . . . was merely figurative and typing out the Christian Churches consisting of both Jews and Gentiles. . . .

In this discovery of that vast and mighty difference between that state of Israel and all other states . . . I shall select some main and principal considerations concerning that state wherein the irreconcilable differences and disproportion may appear.

First, I shall consider the very land and country of Canaan itself, and present some considerations proving it to be a nonesuch.

First, this land was spied out and chosen by the Lord out of all the countries of the world to be the seat of His Church and people.

But now there is no respect of earth, of places, or countries with the Lord. . . .

While that national state of the Church of the Jews remained, the tribes were bound to go up to Jerusalem to worship. But now, in every nation, . . . he that fears God and works righteousness is accepted

Roger Williams, *The Bloudy Tenent, of Persecution, for cause of Conscience* (1644), pp. 316-20, 330.

with Him. This, then, appeared in that large commission of the Lord Jesus to His first ministers: go unto all nations, and not only into Canaan, to carry tidings of mercy, etc. . . .

Fourthly, this land [Canaan], this earth, was an holy land, ceremonially and typically holy fields, gardens, orchards, houses, etc., which holiness the world knows not now in one land, or country, house, field, garden, etc., one above another. . . .

Fifthly, the Lord expressly calls it [Canaan] His own land . . . a term proper unto spiritual Canaan . . . .

But now the partition wall is broken down, and in respect of the Lord's special property to one country more than another, what difference between Asia and Africa, between Europe and America, between England and Turkey, London and Constantinople? . . .

But now Jerusalem from above is not material and earthly, but spiritual. . . .

Peace. It seems (dear Truth) a mighty gulf between that people and nation and the nations of the world then extant and ever since.

Truth. As sure as the blessed substance to all those shadows, Christ Jesus, is come, so unmatchable and never to be paralleled by any national state that was Israel in the figure or shadow.

And yet, the Israel of God now, the regenerate or newborn, the circumcised in heart by repentance and mortification, who willingly submit unto the Lord Jesus as their only King and Head, may fitly parallel and answer that Israel in the [Old Testament] type, without such danger of hypocrisy, of such horrible profanations, and of firing the civil state in such bloody combustions as all ages have brought forth upon this compelling a whole nation or kingdom to be the antitype of Israel. . . .

The Precedent of the Mosaic Laws

Roger Williams

Truth. Moses in the Old Testament was Christ's servant, yet Moses being but a servant, dispensed his power by carnal rites and ceremonies, laws, rewards, and punishments in that holy nation and that one land of Canaan. But when the Lord Jesus, the Son and Lord Himself, was come to bring the truth and life and substance of all those shadows, to break down the partition wall between Jew and Gentile, and to establish the Christian worship and kingdom in all nations of the world, Master Cotton will never prove from any of the books and institutions of the New Testament that unto those spiritual remedies appointed by Christ Jesus against spiritual maladies, He added the help of the carnal sword.

Peace. But Christ (said Master Cotton) never abrogated the carnal sword in the New [Testament] which He appointed in the Old Testament, and the reason of the [Mosaic] law, to wit, an offense of thrusting away from the Lord is perpetual.

Truth. If it appear (as evidently it does) that this King (Jesus, the King of Israel) wears His sword (the antitype of the Kings of Israel, their swords) in His mouth . . . then the answer is as clear as the sun that scatters the clouds and darkness of the night. . . .

For Master Cotton knows the profession of the Lord Jesus (John 18:36) that His kingdom was not earthly, and, therefore, His sword cannot be earthly. Master Cotton knows that Christ Jesus commanded a sword to be put up when it was drawn in the cause of Christ, and added a dreadful threatening: that all that take the sword (that is the carnal sword for His cause) shall perish by it. . . .

Roger Williams, *The Bloody Tenent yet more Bloody* (1652), pp. 185-86, 198, 245, 393, 450-51.

Instead of fire and sword and stoning the [religious] opposites, instead of imprisonment, banishment, death, He has appointed exhortations, reprehensions, denunciations, excommunications, and together with preaching, patient waiting, if God peradventure will give repentance. . . .

Let Master Cotton produce such a miraculous nation or people . . . so brought out of the land of Egypt into covenant with God, etc., and I shall readily grant that seducers of such a people from such a God are worthy to die a thousand deaths. But if Master Cotton will now tell me that the Christian, Congregational Church is the Israel of God, and the coming forth [out] of Egypt is now mystical and spiritual, why will he not content himself with a mystical and spiritual death to be inflicted upon him that shall seduce an Israelite from the Lord, his God? . . .

As much as the shadow of a man fall short of a man himself, so did all their ordinances (which were but shadows of spiritual things to come) fall short of that bright enjoyment of Christ Jesus, and spiritual and heavenly things in Him, now brought to light by Christ Jesus in the Gospel or New Testament. . . .

To make the shadows of the Old Testament and the substance and body of the New all one, is but to confound and mingle heaven and earth together, for the state of the [Mosaic] law was ceremonial and figurative, having a worldly tabernacle, with vanishing and beggarly rudiments. . . .

How can Mr. Cotton then deny, but that the weapons of this people [of Israel in the Old Testament], their punishments and rewards, etc. (so far as concern this their mixed figurative and typical state), were figurative and ceremonial also? And so not parts of moral, civil righteousness, or common to all other nations and peoples in the world . . . .

The Old Testament Is of Eternal Force

John Cotton

Ceremonial laws were generally typical. Not so Moses his Judicials, especially those which had in them moral equity.

It is moral equity that blasphemers and apostate idolaters, seducing others to idolatry, should be put to death. . . . But the external equity of that judicial law of Moses was of moral force and binds all Princes to express that zeal and indignation, both against blasphemy, in such as fall under their just power . . . , and against seduction to idolatry . . . .

And, therefore, it cannot truly be said that the Lord Jesus never appointed the civil sword for a remedy in such a case. For He did expressly appoint it in the Old Testament; nor did He ever abrogate it in the New. The reason of the law (which is the life of the law) is of eternal force and equity in all ages. . . . The reason is of moral, that is, of universal and perpetual equity, to put to death any apostate, seducing idolater, or heretic, who seeks to thrust away the souls of God's people from the Lord their God. . . .

Did ever any apostle or evangelist make the judicial laws of Moses concerning life and death ceremonial or typical? Time was when human inventions in God's worship were accounted superstition; but now human inventions in doctrine may pass for current Evangelical divinity.

It is true the Son of Righteousness has set up another church, ministry, and worship. But did He ever set up another civil righteousness? Or a magistrate to walk by another rule of righteousness than that which God gave by Moses? If it be true that Christ gave no

John Cotton, *The Bloudy Tenent, Washed* (1647), pp. 55, 67, 177-78, 181-82, 193.

express ordinance, precept, or precedent of killing men by material swords for religion's sake, it is as true that neither did He for any breach of civil justice, no not for murder nor adultery. Which makes it, therefore, evident that seeing He has expressly authorized civil magistracy in the New Testament and has given no express laws or rules of righteousness for them to walk by in administration of civil justice, therefore, either He leaves them to act and rule without a rule (which derogates from the perfection of Scripture), or else they must fetch their rules of righteousness from the law of Moses and from the prophets who have expounded Him in the Old Testament. . . .

For since God laid this charge upon magistrates in the Old Testament to punish seducers and the Lord Jesus never took this charge off in the New Testament, who is this Discusser [Williams] that he should account Paul himself, or an Angel from heaven, accursed, that should leave this charge still upon magistrates which God laid on and Christ never took off? . . .

For Christ came not to destroy the law of Moses (Matthew 5: 17). . . .

No, nor did He come to destroy the judicial laws, such of them as are of moral equity. Or else, the conscience of the civil magistrate could never do any act of civil justice out of faith, because he should have no word of God to be the grounds of his action if the laws of judgment in the Old Testament were abrogated and none extant in the New. . . .

Points of Theology and the Unlawfulness of Persecution

Roger Williams

Peace. Yea, but it is said that the blind Pharisees, misguiding the subjects of a civil state, greatly sin against a civil state and, therefore, justly suffer civil punishment; for shall the civil magistrate take care of outsides only, to wit, of the bodies of men, and not of souls, in laboring to procure their everlasting welfare?

Truth. I answer, it is a truth, the mischief of a blind Pharisee's blind guidance is greater than if he acted treasons, murders, etc.; and the loss of one soul by his seduction is a greater mischief than if he blew up parliaments and cut the throats of Kings or Emperors, so precious is that invaluable jewel of a soul, above all the present lives and bodies of all the men in the world! And, therefore, a firm justice calling for [an] eye for eye, tooth for tooth, life for life, calls also for soul for soul, which the blind-guiding, seducing Pharisee shall surely pay in that dreadful ditch which the Lord Jesus speaks of; but this sentence against him the Lord Jesus only pronounces in His Church, His spiritual judicature, and executes this sentence in part at present and hereafter to all eternity. Such a sentence no civil judge can pass, such a death no civil sword can inflict.

I answer, secondly, dead men cannot be infected, the civil state, the world, being in a natural state dead in sin (whatever be the state religion unto which persons are forced), it is impossible it should be infected. Indeed, the living, the believing, the church and spiritual state, that and that only is capable of infection. . . .

So here, whatever be the soul infection breathed out from the lying lips of a plague-sick Pharisee, yet . . . not one elect or chosen of God shall perish. God's sheep are safe in His eternal hand and

Roger Williams, *The Bloudy Tenent, of Persecution, for cause of Conscience* (1644), pp. 125-26, 137-39, 208-209, 258-59.

counsel, and He that knows His material, knows also His mystical stars, their numbers, and calls them every one by name; none falls into the ditch on the blind Pharisee's back, but such as were ordained to that condemnation, both guide and followers. . . .

Peace. But it has been thought, or said, shall oppositions against the truth escape unpunished? Will they not prove mischievous, etc.?

Truth. I answer (as before), concerning the blind guides (in case there be no civil offense committed), the magistrates and all men that by the mercy of God to themselves discern the misery of such [religious] opposites, have cause to lament and bewail that fearful condition wherein such are entangled, to wit, in the snares and chains of Satan, with which they are so invincibly caught and held that no power in heaven or earth, but the right hand of the Lord in the meek and gentle dispensing of the word of truth, can release and acquit them. . . .

A carnal weapon or sword of steel may produce a carnal repentance, a show, an outside, an [religious] uniformity through a state or kingdom. . . .

Accordingly, an unbelieving soul, being dead in sin (although he be changed from one worship to another, like a dead man shifted into several changes of apparel), cannot please God; and, consequently, whatever such an unbelieving and unregenerate person acts in worship or religion, it is but sin. . . .

Peace. I add, that a civil sword . . . is so far from bringing or helping forward an opposite in religion to repentance that magistrates sin grievously against the work of God and blood of souls by such proceedings [of persecution]. Because as (commonly) the sufferings of false and anti-Christian teachers harden their followers, who, being blind by this means, are occasioned to tumble into the ditch of hell after their blind leaders with more inflamed zeal of lying confidence. So, secondly, violence and a sword of steel begets such an impression in the sufferers that, certainly, they conclude (as, indeed, that religion cannot be true which needs such instruments of violence to uphold it so) that persecutors are far from soft and gentle commiseration of the blindness of others. . . .

Truth. The souls of all men in the world are either naturally dead in sin or alive in Christ. If dead in sin, no man can kill them, no more than he can kill a dead man. Nor is it a false teacher or false religion that can so much prevent the means of spiritual life, as one of these two: Either the force of a material sword, imprisoning the souls of men in a state or national religion, ministry, or worship. Or, secondly, civil wars and combustions for religion's sake, whereby men are immediately cut off without any longer means of repentance.

Now, again, for the souls that are alive in Christ, He has graciously appointed ordinances powerfully sufficient to maintain and cherish that life. . . .

Secondly, the soul once alive in Christ is like Christ Himself, alive forever, and cannot die a spiritual death. . . .

Peace. Methinks I discern a three-fold guilt to lie upon such civil powers as impose upon and enforce the conscience . . . either to depart from that worship which it is persuaded of, or to any exercise or worship which it has not faith in.

First, of an appearance of that Arminian, Popish doctrine of free will, as if it lay in their own power and ability to believe upon the magistrate's command, since it is confessed that what is submitted to by any without faith it is sin, be it never so true and holy.

Secondly, since God only opens the heart and works the will, it seems to be an high presumption to suppose that together with a command restraining from, or constraining to, worship, that God is also to be forced or commanded to give faith to open the heart to incline the will, etc.

Thirdly, a guilt of the hypocrisy of their subjects and people in forcing them to act and practice in matters of religion and worship against the doubts and checks of their consciences, causing their bodies to worship when their souls are far off, to draw near with their lips, their hearts being far off, etc. . . .

source 19

Predestination Reconciled with Persecution

John Cotton

Discusser [Roger Williams]

But dead men cannot die, nor be infected. Natural men, the civil state, the world, are dead in sin, etc.

Defender [John Cotton]

Reply 1. Dead men may be made worse by corrupt teachers . . . . And, therefore, such as so corrupt them are worthy in a way of due proceeding of a two-fold death.

Reply 2. Such as [who are not saints but] profess the truth of the doctrine and worship of Christ, they live a kind of spiritual life, though not such as accompanies salvation. . . . And, therefore, it is not true "that such as being in a natural state are dead in sin, and cannot be infected nor die again."

Discusser [Roger Williams]

As in the common infection of the plague, so in the infection of heresy, none can be struck deadly, but whom God has thereunto ordained, etc.

Defender [John Cotton]

Reply 1. No more can any man be murdered but whom God has ordained thereunto. But it is a profane sacrilege to excuse or alleviate the punishment of sin by God's eternal predestination.

John Cotton, *The Bloudy Tenent, Washed* (1647), pp. 65, 83, 176.

Reply 2. The Discusser himself acknowledges "that though in a common plague or infection, none are smitten or die, but such as are ordained thereunto," yet it is not only every man's duty, but the common duty of the magistrates, to prevent infection and to preserve the common health of the place by removing infectious persons into solitary tabernacles. . . .

Yet better a dead soul be dead in body as well as in spirit, than to live and be lively in the flesh, to murder many precious souls by the magistrate's indulgence. And better he die without faith, than to live to seduce many honest minds to depart from the faith. . . .

It is an high presumptuous tempting of God, and wanton treading under foot the precious souls of men for whom Christ died, to wound and (as much as in us lies) to kill the souls of men upon pretence the Lord can save them and raise them again by His all-sufficient grace. It is a putting of fear where none is that the punishment of obstinate, seducing "heretics with the material sword is the imprisoning of the souls of men to a national religion." For if the religion of the nation be good, it is no imprisonment; if naught, there should be no punishment. And it is a like causeless fear that the cutting off of heretics "will cut off men immediately without any longer means of repentance." For if they belong to God, God will give them repentance before they go hence; but whether they belong to God or not, the revealed will of God is fulfilled in their just execution. . . .

source 20

The Lessons of History Reject Persecution

Roger Williams

Truth. First, if the civil magistrates be Christians or members of the church . . . then I say as before, they are bound by this command of Christ to suffer opposition to their doctrine with meekness and gentleness, and to be so far from striving to subdue their [religious] opposites with the civil sword that they are bound with patience and meekness to wait if God peradventure will please to grant repentance unto their [religious] opposites. . . .

Secondly, . . . True it is the sword may make . . . a whole nation of hypocrites. But to recover a soul from Satan by repentance, and to bring them from anti-Christian doctrine or worship to the doctrine or worship Christian . . . , that alone works the all-powerful God, by the sword of the spirit in the hand of His spiritual officers.

What a most woeful proof hereof have the nations of the earth given in all ages? And to seek no further than our native soil [England], within a few scores of years, how many wonderful changes in religion has the whole kingdom made according to the change of the governors thereof in the several religions which they themselves embraced! Henry VII finds and leaves the kingdom absolutely Popish. Henry VIII casts it into a mold half-Popish, half-Protestant. Edward VI brings forth an edition all Protestant. Queen Mary, within [a] few years, defaces Edward VI's work and renders the kingdom (after her grandfather, Henry VII, his pattern) all Popish. Mary's short life and [established] religion end together. And Elizabeth revives her brother Edward VI's model, all Protestant. . . .

Peace. It has been England's sinful shame to fashion and change

Roger Williams, *The Bloudy Tenent, of Persecution, for cause of Conscience* (1644), pp. 135-37, 142.

its garments and religions with wondrous ease and lightness as a higher power, a stronger sword has prevailed. . . .

Truth. And I ask whether or not such as may hold forth other worships or religions (Jews, Turks, or anti-Christians), may not be peaceable and quiet subjects, loving and helpful neighbors, fair and just dealers, true and loyal to the civil government? It is clear they may from all reason and experience in many flourishing cities and kingdoms of the world, and so offend not against the civil state and peace; nor incur the punishment of the civil sword, notwithstanding that in spiritual and mystical account they are ravenous and greedy wolves. . . .

History Does Not Excuse Dissent

John Cotton

What the Kings and Queens of England have done in former or later times, either by violent persecution of the truth or in preposterous maintenance of the truth, we have cause rather to bewail it . . . than to justify it; as also bewail the like vanity, justly complained of in sundry of our English nation, to be as ready to change the fashion of their religion as of their raiment. And yet, he [Williams] cannot be ignorant that the Lord has chosen to Himself sundry faithful witnesses out of that nation who have continued steadfast unto the death in the profession of the truth, and have not been carried away, either with the fear of civil sword, or with the deceitful insinuations of unstable but seducing teachers, to depart from the simplicity and truth of the Gospel. But howsoever woeful and wonderful changes have been made of religion in England in the reign of four or five Princes, yet it is no more than befell the Church of Judah [in the Old Testament]. . . . Better some vicissitudes in religion than a constant continuance in idolatry and Popery by Princes referring all causes of religion to church men. . . .

John Cotton, *The Bloudy Tenent, Washed* (1647), p. 82.

source 22

Persecution Brings Civil Chaos

Roger Williams

Peace. Dear *Truth,* I have two sad complaints:

First, the most sober of your witnesses that dare to plead your cause, how are they charged to be my enemies, contentious, turbulent, seditious?

Secondly, your enemies, though they speak and rail against you, though they outrageously pursue, imprison, banish, kill your faithful witnesses, yet how is all colored over for "justice against the heretics"? Yea, if they kindle coals and blow the flames of devouring wars that leave neither spiritual nor civil state, but burn up branch and root, yet how do all pretend an holy war? He that kills, and he that is killed, they both cry out it is for God and for their conscience.

It is true, nor one nor other seldom dare to plead the mighty Prince, Christ Jesus, for their author; yet both (both Protestant and Papist) pretend they have spoken with Moses and the Prophets, who all, say they, before Christ came allowed such holy persecutions, holy wars, against the enemies of holy church.

Truth. Dear *Peace,* . . . your dearest sons, most like their mother, peace-keeping, peace-making sons of God, have borne and still must bear the blurs of troublers of Israel, and turners of the world upside down. . . .

Yet strife must be distinguished: It is necessary or unnecessary, godly or ungodly, Christian or unchristian, etc.

It is unnecessary, unlawful, dishonorable, ungodly, unchristian in most cases in the world [to persecute men for their faith], for there is

Roger Williams, *The Bloudy Tenent, of Persecution, for cause of Conscience* (1644), pp. 58-61, 80-81.

a possibility of keeping sweet peace in most cases, and if it be possible, it is the express command of God that peace be kept. . . .

What fearful cries within these twenty years of hundreds [of] thousands, men, women, children, fathers, mothers, husbands, wives, brethren, sisters, old and young, high and low, plundered, ravished, slaughtered, murdered, famished? And hence these cries, that men fling away the spiritual sword and spiritual artillery (in spiritual and religious causes) and rather trust for the suppressing of each other's God, conscience, and religion . . . to an arm of flesh and sword of steel. . . .

. . . breach of civil peace may arise when false and idolatrous practices are held forth, and yet no breach of civil peace from the doctrine or practice or the manner of holding forth, but from that wrong and preposterous way of suppressing, preventing, and extinguishing such doctrines or practices by weapons of wrath and blood, whips, stocks, imprisonment, banishment, death, etc., by which men commonly are persuaded to convert heretics and to cast out unclean spirits. . . .

Hence the town is in an uproar, and the country takes the alarm to expel that fog or mist of error, heresy, blasphemy (as it is supposed [effective]), with swords or guns; whereas, it is light alone, even light from the bright, shining Son of Righteousness, which is able in the soul and consciences of men to dispel and scatter such fogs and darkness.

Hence the sons of men disquiet themselves in vain, and unmercifully disquiet others . . . .

source 23

Dissent Is Dangerous

John Cotton

When the wrath of God is kindled against a state for corruption of religion, He pours out His judgments against them by degrees; first upon the common sort of people, then upon church officers, and then upon the principal rulers and lights of that state. . . .

It may serve then to be a watchword and warning to the common sort of Christians. First, look you to it, men and brethren and beloved in Christ Jesus, look you to it tenderly and seriously, that neither doctrine, nor worship of God, nor church government be corrupt to your best discerning, but preserved by diligent examination of all things, according to the pattern shown in the word as it has been hitherto held forth to you. . . . Let church officers look to it, and let civil magistrates see to it, it is their calling to look to worship and government in their time and place; though that be true, they must look to it, and God will require it else at their hand, yet, if you look not to it, the wrath of God will be poured out upon you. . . .

Has the Lord begun to smite the common state . . . in the scarcities of monies? Brethren, do you think it is not a judgment of God? Is not the silver and gold His? And has He it not for this state as well as for others, if we had not some ways provoked Him? . . . Has not the Lord blasted us, because we grew cold-hearted and formal in church fellowship, and confident and warm and bold-hearted in matters pertaining to ourselves and to the world, and in matters that tended only to tumult? What then? In such a case marvel not if the Lord send forth a vial of His wrath upon us, and curse our blessings. . . .

John Cotton, *Powring out of the Seven Vials* (1642), Part 4, pp. 10, 14-15, 21-22.

source 24

Civil Peace Demands Spiritual Purity

John Cotton

But what is then the peace of the city or country? Is it not . . . the tranquility of order in every society wherein the public weal of the city or country is concerned? And is it not the proper work of the civil magistrate to preserve the civil peace, and to prevent or reform the disturbance of the tranquility or peace of any such societies in whose peace the peace or weal of the city or society is concerned? Suppose a society of merchants, or clothiers, or fishmongers, or drapers, or the like. If the weal of the city or country be concerned in these (as it is much concerned in them all), is it not for the safety of the civil state to suffer any of these so to be disturbed, as wholly to break up and to be dissolved. . . .

If by peace be meant (as in Scripture language it is) all welfare, it would argue a man that lives in the world [not] to be too much ignorant of the state of the world, to say: "that in the breaking up and dissolving of such particular societies the peace of the city or country is not in the least measure impaired or disturbed. . . ."

Now, then, if all these particular societies and several companies of trades, they and their peace and welfare, do much concern the welfare and peace of the city and country, and, therefore, it behooves the civil government to provide for their peace and welfare, I demand, whether the church also (which is a particular society of Christians), whether, I say, the peace and welfare of it do not concern the peace and welfare of the city or country where they live?

If it be denied, it is easily proven.

First, David said, they shall prosper that love the peace of Jerusalem and seek the good of it. And Solomon said, "where the righteous

John Cotton, *The Bloudy Tenent, Washed* (1647), pp. 10-13.

rejoice there is great glory." And what is the church, but a congregation of righteous men? If the rejoicing of the church be the glory of a nation, surely the disturbing and distracting and dissolving of the church is the shame and confusion of a nation.

2. Consider the excellency and preeminence of the church above all other societies. . . . The world and all societies of it are for the church. The world would not subsist but for the church; nor any country in the world but for the service of the church. And can the church then break up into pieces and dissolve into nothing, and yet the peace and welfare of the city not in the least measure impaired or disturbed?

3. It is a matter of just displeasure to God and sad grief of heart to the church when civil states look at the estate of the church as of little or no concernment to themselves. . . .

It is true where the church is not cities and towns may enjoy some measure of civil peace, yea, and flourish in outward prosperity for a time through the patience and bounty and long sufferance of God. . . . But when the church comes to be planted among them, if then civil states do neglect them and suffer the churches to corrupt and annoy themselves by pollutions in religion, the staff of the peace of the commonwealth will soon be broken as the purity of religion is broken in the churches. . . .

Though the peace of the country or commonwealth be civil and human, yet it is distracted and cut off by disturbing the spiritual purity and peace of the church. . . .

The Controversy Begins in England

Thomas Goodwin, *et al.*

And we do . . . here publicly profess, we believe the [religious] truth to lie and consist in a middle way betwixt that which is falsely charged on us, Brownism [Separatism]; and that which is the contention of these times, the authoritative Presbyterian government, in all the subordinations and proceedings of it. . . .

But it is sufficiently known that in all points of doctrine . . . our judgments have still concurred with the greatest part of our [Presbyterian] brethren . . . . And in matters of [church] discipline . . . when our judgments cannot in all things concur with others . . . yet we are so far from holding up the differences that occur, or making the breaches greater or wider, that we endeavor upon all such occasions to grant and yield . . . to the utmost latitude of our light and consciences. . . . And further, when matters by discussion are brought to the smallest dissent that may be, we have hitherto been found to be no backward urgers unto a temper (not only in things that have concerned our own consciences, but when of others also) such as may suit and tend to union as well as searching out of truth; judging this to be as great and useful an end of synods and assemblies, as a curious and exact discussion of all sorts of lesser differences with binding determination of truth one way. . . .

Thomas Goodwin, *et. al.*, *An Apologeticall Narration, Humbly submitted to the Honourable Houses of Parliament* (London: 1644), pp. 24, 28-30.

An Appeal for Toleration

William Walwyn

Having heretofore met with *An Apologeticall Narration* of Thomas Goodwin, Philip Nye, Sidrach Simpson, Jeremiah Burroughs, William Bridge, I did with gladness of heart undertake the reading thereof, expecting therein to find such general reasons for the justification of themselves to the world as would have justified all the separation [Separatists], and so have removed by one discourse those prejudices and misapprehensions which even good men have of that harmless and well-meaning sort of people. But finding contrary to that expectation that their *Apology* therein [was] for themselves and their toleration was grounded rather upon a remonstrance of the nearness between them and the Presbyterian, being one in doctrine with them and very little differing from them in discipline, how they had been tolerated by other Presbyter churches . . . .

Finding to my heart's grief, the Separatists thus left in the lurch, and likely to be exposed to greater dangers than ever by the endeavors of these men, my heart abounded with grief. . . . Methinks every man is bound in conscience to speak and do what he can in behalf of such a harmless people as these. What though you are no Separatist (as I myself am none) the love of God appears most in doing good for others. That love which aims only at itself, those endeavors which would procure liberty only to themselves, can best be called but self-love and self-respect. It is common freedom every man ought to aim at, which is every man's peculiar right so far as it is not prejudicial to the common. Now because little can be done in their behalf unless liberty

William Walwyn, *The Compassionate Samaritane Unbinding The Conscience, and powring Oyle into the wounds which have been made upon the Separation.* . . . (London: 1644), pp. 1-5.

of conscience be allowed for every man or sort of men to worship God in that way and perform Christ's ordinances in that manner as shall appear to them most agreeable to God's word, and no man be punished or discountenanced by authority for his opinion unless it be dangerous to the state, I have endeavored in this discourse to make appear, by the best reason I have, that every man ought to have liberty of conscience of what opinion soever, with the caution above named. . . .

Wholesome Severity Reconciled
with Christian Liberty

George Gillespie

. . . liberty of heresy and schism is no part of the liberty of conscience which Christ has purchased to us at so dear a rate. . . .

Under these fair colors and handsome pretexts do sectaries infuse their poison, I mean their pernicious, God-provoking, truth-defacing, church-ruinating, and state-shaking toleration. The plain English of the question is this: Whether the Christian magistrate be keeper of both tables [of the Ten Commandments]; whether he ought to suppress his own enemies, but not God's enemies, and preserve his own ordinances but not Christ's ordinances from violation; whether the troublers of Israel may be troubled. . . . I have endeavored in this following discourse to vindicate the lawful, yea, necessary, use of the coercive power of the Christian magistrate in suppressing and punishing heretics and sectaries. . . .

The ceremonial law [of the Old Testament] was written for our learning, that we might know the fulfilling of all those types, but the judicial law [of Moses] was not typical. . . .

Though we have clear and full Scriptures in the New Testament for abolishing the ceremonial law, yet we nowhere read in all the New Testament of the abolishing of the judicial law [of Moses], so far as it did concern the punishing of sins against the moral law, of which heresy and seducing of souls is one, and a great one. . . .

This doctrine of the magistrate's coercive power makes many to stumble at the Presbyterian reformation as a bloody reformation . . . . We have not so learned Christ . . . . It is my soul's desire that the

George Gillespie, *Wholesome Severity Reconciled with Christian Liberty. Or, The True Resolution of a present Controversy concerning Liberty of Conscience.* . . . (London: 1645), preface and pp. 8, 18-20.

secular coercive power may be put forth upon those only who can by no other means be reclaimed, and who can be no longer spared without a visible rupture in the church and the manifest danger of seducing and misleading many souls. A Presbytery is not so ill a neighbor that no man who has the least differing opinion may live beside it.

But this objection [of persecution] does as much strike against the New England government as against the government of the neighboring reformed churches [of Scotland]. For in New England there has been severity enough (to say no worse) used against heretics and schismatics. And here I must appeal [to] the consciences of those who now plead so much for liberty of conscience and toleration in this kingdom, were they able to root out the Presbyterians and their way, and could find civil authority inclinable to put forth the coercive power against it, whether in that case would they not say that the magistrate may repress it by strong hand, if it cannot be otherwise repressed. . . . Now I assume there are some who plead for liberty of conscience who profess that they are certain and fully assured, upon demonstrative proofs, that the Presbyterian way is not from God, nor according to the mind of Jesus Christ . . . . Therefore, according to their [Congregational] principles they must allow of the putting forth of the civil coercive power against the Presbyterian way. And if so, what a grand imposture is this? What a deceiving of the world? What a mocking of the Parliament and of the kingdom? To plead generally for liberty of conscience, when they intend only liberty to themselves, not to others that are opposite to them. . . .

A Presbyterian Wants Religious Uniformity

Thomas Edwards

As for the matter itself contained in the close of your book—a toleration of Independent [Congregational] churches and government —the scope and last end of this *Apology*, whereunto tends all the artifice and fallacies in the composure of it, I shall lay down some reasons and grounds against it. . . .

1. A toleration of Independent [Congregational] churches and government with their opinions and practice is against the magistrate's duty laid down in Scripture; but for the magistrates by good laws to command and require obedience to the government and reformation upon good grounds judged to be according to the word of God, and so established [by law], is lawful and their duties. . . .

2. The toleration desired is against the Solemn League and Covenant for reformation taken by the Parliament [with Scotland] . . . .

3. A toleration is against the nature of reformation; a reformation and a toleration are diametrically opposite . . . .

4. A toleration of men in their errors, this pretended liberty of conscience, is against the judgment of the greatest lights in the church, both ancient and modern. . . .

And to the judgment of the Fathers [of Christianity] and the modern writers on this point, I will add the judgment of the divines of New England, who are against the toleration of any church government and way but one. . . . And so in New England they will not suffer Brownists, Anabaptists, Antinomians. Mr. Cotton, the greatest divine in New England and a precious man, is against tolerations, and holds that men may be punished for their consciences, as will appear

Thomas Edwards, *Antapologia: Or, a Full Answer to the Apologeticall Narration.* . . . (London: 1644), pp. 280-92, 299, 302-304.

by his *Letter* to Mr. Williams, and Mr. Williams' *Answer* (both printed), and his *Exposition on the Vials,* wherein he answers an objection: "But you will say conscience should not be forced, etc." He answers: "Why do you think heretics were not as conscionable in the Old Testament as now? . . ."

5. The magistrate's toleration of errors and new opinions is a kind of invitation to them, a temptation, and occasion of many falling who otherwise never would, a snare to many, a stumbling block laid before the weak, the leaving a pit or well uncovered, an opportunity for Satan . . . .

6. A toleration of one or more different ways of churches and church government from the church and church government established [by law], will be to this kingdom very mischievous, pernicious and destructive, in regard of the effects and consequences of it. . . . Different forms of churches and church government in one state must needs lay a foundation of strife and division therein. It is the admitting of a seed of perpetual division within itself, an opening a sluice to let in strife and contentions in all places public and private, church and commonwealth, in parliaments, corporations, among the ministers, in families. . . .

A toleration will spoil any church and government; if Presbyterian government be settled, and a toleration given in this land, that will mar all. . . .

Whether would you have a toleration granted in the general, and indifferently, for all consciences, sects, and opinions; or only for some sort of opinions. I suppose, being wise men, you will not express yourselves for a toleration in the first sense, but in the latter. I desire to know of you, then, what limits and bounds you will set, and where the Parliament shall stop, and what rules you will give for this? As first, whether the limitation shall be a toleration only for all different forms of church government and order, so long as they agree in doctrine with the church established [by law], and are orthodox? . . . Or, secondly, would you have a toleration in points of doctrine too, namely, in lesser differences? I desire to know what you will make the rule and measure of those lesser differences? . . . Now in the close of my discourse against toleration, I take the humble boldness to represent to the honorable houses of Parliament that it is the magistrate's duty not to suffer schisms, heresies, and other errors to grow and increase in the church. . . . One of the great services Princes and Parliament perform to Christ in reference to their great and high calling consists in making laws for the observing the worship and government of His House, and by laws prohibiting all other worships and governments. And I humbly beseech the Parliament seriously to consider the depths of Satan in this design of a toleration, how this is now his last plot and design, and by it would undermine and frustrate the whole work of reformation intended. It is his masterpiece for England . . . . In a word, could the Devil effect a toleration, he would think he had gained well by the reformation . . . .

Persecution Condemned

Richard Overton

1. *Mr. Sovereignty of Christ.* Gentlemen, our Lord of Lords . . . has by the price of His blood, constituted Himself sole Head and King forever over the consciences of men and, therefore, he charges His householders, the kings of the earth, to let the tares and the wheat grow together in the field of the world until the harvest, the day of judgment; therefore, this malefactor Persecution, in my judgment, being in his inclinations and actions altogether adverse thereto, is an arch-traitor to the prerogative-royal of Jesus Christ over the consciences of men, and, therefore, lawfully and justly charged with this bill [of guilt].

2. *Mr. Power of Parliaments.* My verdict, Mr. Foreman, is that persecution for conscience is inconsistent with the sovereignty of kingdoms, for it divides their powers one against another, and in themselves occasions murmurings, grutchings, and repinings, which in time break forth into conspiracies, rebellions, insurrections, etc., as well to the prejudice of sovereignty, as to the ruin of the subject. . . .

4. *Mr. National-Strength.* Mr. Foreman, I conceive that you cannot be insensible that the national strength of kingdoms and peoples consists in the general peace . . . wherefore, to foster this malefactor [persecution] among a people, is to render the strength of a kingdom to ruin, for he is a constant sower of division, emulation, hatred, etc., among them. . . .

5. *Mr. Settled-Peace.* Mr. Foreman, by reason of persecution for conscience, I can find no absolute acceptance in any kingdom or nation

Richard Overton, *The Araignement of Mr. Persecution: Presented to the Consideration of the House of Commons.* . . . (London: 1645), pp. 4-6, 19-20, 26-27.

throughout Christendom. For he so poisons all national pacifications, leagues, and covenants, that their peace changes with their religion. . . .

7. *Mr. United-Provinces* [Netherlands]. Mr. Foreman, whosoever reads the history of the United Provinces, and considers their wonderful preservation, flourishing state, and prosperity they enjoy, notwithstanding their waging of continual war with a foreign enemy [Spain], may clearly perceive the great mercy of God upon a nation and a people, that in tender to the consciences one of another, exclude, banish, and extirpate persecution out of their territories. . . .

8. *Mr. Desolate-Germany.* Mr. Foreman, those that doubt of the truth . . . let them but look upon the German desolations, depopulations, war, famine, and pestilence . . . .

10. *Mr. National-Wealth.* Mr. Foreman, that which is the ruin of national wealth is destructive to the very being and continuance of nations, kingdoms, and states; for it brings devastation and depopulation thereof, and so not to be suffered. But this persecution for conscience stirs up wars and bloodshed in nations, kingdoms, and states, which consumes their wealth, devours their fruit, burns and destroys their cities, towns, and villages, and throws all into a wilderness. . . .

Sir John Presbyter.

My Lord, my reasons against liberty of conscience . . . .

Because it is against the greatest lights in the church, both ancient and modern, as Augustine, Ambrose, Calvin, . . . likewise the judgment of the divines of New England are against the toleration of any church government and way but one; they will not suffer Brownists, Anabaptists, etc. Mr. Cotton, the greatest divine in New England and a precious man, is against toleration, and holds that men may be punished for their consciences, as will appear by his *Letter to* Mr. Williams. Ergo:

I. *Reason.* Presbyterian government is unlawful, because Mr. Cotton condemns it . . . .

Gospel. Mr. Foreman, whereas it is . . . urged that the Kings of the Gentiles have equal power with the Kings of Israel of old, understand that their supremacy was but for a time . . . . The old covenant [in the Old Testament] was over the old man . . . . The new covenant [in the New Testament] is over the new man . . . . Therefore, as the resurrection cannot possibly be but by Christ, so the penalty [in religious matters] cannot possibly be by other; it is out of the sphere of this world, therefore, out of the power of the Princes of this world; as they cannot be mediators of the New Testament, so they cannot be punishers therein. Therefore, to punish the [religious] offenders therein, is to attempt the throne of Christ, and usurp . . . His mediatorship. Therefore, has He referred the contemners of His Gospel until the judgment of the last day. . . .

A New England Narrative

John Clarke

It came to pass that we three [John Clarke, Obadiah Holmes, John Crandall] . . . came into the Massachusetts Bay upon the 16th day of the 5th month, 1651; and upon the 19th of the same, upon occasion of business, we came into a town in the same [Massachusetts] Bay called Lynn, where we lodged at a blind man's house, near two miles out of the town, by name William Witter . . . . I was imparting [on religious matters] to my companions in the house where I lodged, and to four or five strangers that came in unexpected after I had begun . . . while I say I was yet speaking, there comes into the house where we were, two constables, who with their clamorous tongues made an interruption in my discourse, and more uncivilly disturbed us than the pursuivants of the Old English [Anglican] bishops were wont to do; telling us that they were come with authority from the magistrate to apprehend us . . . .

[The three Baptists were arrested and taken to Boston for sentencing.]

After my sentence [of a fine] was read, the sentences of the other two were likewise pronounced; the sentence of Obadiah Holmes was to pay by the aforesaid time thirty pounds, or be well whipped; and the sentence of John Crandall was to pay five pounds, or be well whipped. This being done, I desired to know whether I might not speak a few things to the court . . . . I said . . . we are strangers and strangers to your laws, and may be transgressors of them before we are aware; we would, therefore, desire this courtesy of you as strangers, that you would show us the law by which we are transgressors. . . . At

John Clarke, *Ill Newes from New England: or A Narrative of New Englands Persecution. . . .* (London: 1652), *Passim.*

length the governor [John Endecott] stepped up, and told us we had
denied Infant Baptism, and being somewhat transported, broke forth and
told me I had deserved death, and said, he "would not have such trash
brought into their jurisdiction." Moreover, he said, "you go up and
down and secretly insinuate into those that are weak, but you cannot
maintain it before our ministers, you may try, and discourse or dispute
with them, etc." To this I had much to reply, but that he commanded
the jailor to take us away. . . .

[Clarke includes in his book a letter by Obadiah Holmes giving
his memoir of what happened.]

Not long after these troubles I came upon occasion of business into
the colony of the Massachusetts with two other brethren, as Brother
Clarke, being one of the two, can inform you, where we three were
apprehended, carried to the prison at Boston, and so to the court, and
were all sentenced. . . . Upon the pronouncing of which as I went
from the bar, I expressed myself in these words: "I bless God I am
counted worthy to suffer for the name of Jesus." Whereupon, John
Wilson, their pastor as they call him, struck me before the judgment
seat, and cursed me, saying: "The curse of God or Jesus go with you."
So we were carried to the prison . . . .

[Holmes would not permit his fine to be paid and was whipped.
The fines imposed on Clarke and Crandall were paid.]

This tragedy being thus enacted in the face of the country, must
needs awaken and rouse up the minds and spirits of many, cause sad
thoughts to arise in their hearts, and to flow forth at their mouths as
men offended to see strangers professing godliness so discourteously
used, for no civil transgression, but merely for conscience, and that
[punishment] by their hands who pretended that liberty of conscience
was also the cause of their flight [to New England] . . . .

Mr. Cotton . . . in his sermon immediately before the court
gave their sentence against Mr. Clarke, Obadiah Holmes, and John
Crandall, affirmed that denying Infant Baptism would overthrow all;
and this was a capital offense, and, therefore, they were foul murderers.
When, therefore, the governor, John Endecott, came into the court to
pass sentence against them, he said thus: "You deserve to die, but this
we agreed upon, that Mr. Clarke shall pay twenty pounds fine, and
Obadiah Holmes thirty pounds fine, and John Crandall five pounds
fine, and to remain in prison until their fines be either paid, or security
given for them, or else they are all of them to be well whipped. . . ."

source 31

Letter to John Cotton and John Wilson

Sir Richard Saltonstall

It does not a little grieve my spirit to hear what sad things are reported daily of your tyranny and persecutions in New England, as that you fine, whip, and imprison men for their consciences. First, you compel such to come into your assemblies . . . . Truly, friends, this your practice of compelling any in matters of worship to do that whereof they are not fully persuaded is to make them sin, for so the Apostle tells us, and many are made hypocrites thereby, conforming in their outward man for fear of punishment. We pray for you and wish you prosperity [in] every way, [and] hoped the Lord would have given you so much light and love there [in New England] that you might have been eyes to God's people here [in England] and not to practice those courses in a wilderness which you went so far to prevent. These rigid ways have laid you very low in the hearts of the saints. I do assure you I have heard them pray in the public assemblies that the Lord would give you meek and humble spirits, not to strive so much for uniformity [of worship] as to keep the unity of the spirit in the bond of peace.

When I was in Holland about the beginning of our [civil] wars, I remember some Christians there then had serious thoughts of planting in New England, desired me to write to the governor thereof to know if those that differ . . . in religion, as Anabaptists, Seekers, Antinomians, and the like might be permitted to live among you. To which I received this short answer from your then governor, Mr.

Sir Richard Saltonstall, Letter to John Cotton and John Wilson [London, 1652], in Thomas Hutchinson, ed., *A Collection of Original Papers Relative to the History of the Colony of Massachusetts* (Boston: 1769), pp. 401-402.

[Thomas] Dudley: "God forbid," said he, "our love for the truth should be grown so cold that we should tolerate errors." And when (for satisfaction of myself and others) I desired to know your grounds, he referred me to the books written here between the Presbyterians and Independents, which if that had been sufficient, I needed not have sent so far to understand the reasons of your practice. I hope you do not assume to yourselves infallibility of judgment, when the most learned of the Apostles confessed he knew but in part and saw but darkly, as through a glass; for God is light, and no further than He does illuminate us can we see, be our parts and learning never so great. Oh, that all those who are brethren, though yet they cannot think and speak the same things, might be of one accord in the Lord. Now the God of patience and consolation grant you to be thus minded toward one another, after the example of Jesus Christ, our blessed Saviour, in whose everlasting arms of protection He leaves you who will never leave to be.

Principles in Practice

John Cotton

My brother Wilson and myself do both of us acknowledge your love. . . . For when the complaints you hear of are against our tyranny and persecutions in fining, whipping, and imprisoning men for their consciences, be pleased to understand we look at such complaints as altogether injurious in respect of ourselves, who had no hand or tongue at all to promote either the coming of the persons you aim at into our assemblies, or their punishment for their carriage there. Righteous judgment will not take up reports, much less reproaches, against the innocent. . . . Yet neither are we so vast in our indulgence or toleration as to think the men you speak of suffered an unjust censure. For one of them (Obadiah Holmes), being an excommunicate person himself out of a church in Plymouth patent, came into this jurisdiction and took upon himself to baptize, which I think himself will not say he was compelled here to perform. And he was not ignorant that the rebaptizing of an elder person—and that by a private person, out of [ministerial] office, and under excommunication—are all of them manifest contestations against the order and government of our churches, established (we know) by God's law and (he knows) by the laws of the country. And we conceive we may safely appeal to the ingenuity of your own judgment, whether it would be tolerated in any civil state for a stranger to come and practice [his faith] contrary to the known principles of their church estate? As for his whipping, it was more voluntarily chosen by him than inflicted on him. His censure by the court was to have paid (as I know) thirty pounds, or else to be whipped. His fine was offered to be paid by friends for him freely;

John Cotton, Letter to Sir Richard Saltonstall, in Thomas Hutchinson, ed., *Collection of Original Papers*, pp. 403-406.

but he chose rather to be whipped. In which case, if his suffering of
stripes was any worship of God at all, surely it could be accounted no
better than will-worship. The other (Mr. Clarke) was wiser in that
point . . . and himself (as I hear) was contented to have it paid for
him, whereupon he was released. . . .

But be pleased to consider this point a little further. You think to
compel men in matter of worship is to make men sin . . . . If the
worship be lawful in itself, the magistrate compelling him to come to
it compels him not to sin; but the sin is in his will that needs to be
compelled to a Christian duty. . . . For a governor to suffer any
within his gates to profane the Sabbath is a sin against the fourth
commandment, both in the private householder and in the magistrate;
and if he requires them to present themselves before the Lord, the
magistrate sins not, nor does the subject sin so great a sin as if he
did refrain to come. . . .

But, say you, "it does but make men hypocrites, to compel men to
conform the outward man for fear of punishment." If it did so, yet
better to be hypocrites than profane persons. Hypocrites give God part
of His due, the outward man, but the profane person gives God
neither outward nor inward man. . . .

Do you think the Lord has crowned the state with so many vic-
tories that they should suffer so many miscreants to pluck the crown
of sovereignty from Christ's head? Some to deny His godhead, some
His manhood, some to acknowledge no Christ, nor heaven, nor hell,
but what is in a man's self? . . . Now God forbid, God from heaven
forbid, that the people and state of England should so ill requite the
Lord Jesus. . . . We believe there is a vast difference between men's
inventions and God's institutions. We fled from men's inventions, to
which we else should have been compelled [in England]; we compel
none to men's inventions.

If our ways ("rigid ways" as you call them) have laid us low
in the hearts of God's people, yea and of the saints (as you style them),
we do not believe it is any part of their saintship. . . .

What you wrote out of Holland to our then Governor, Mr.
[Thomas] Dudley, in behalf of Anabaptists, Antinomians, Seekers, and
the like, it seems met with a short answer from him, but zealous. . . .
Nevertheless, I tell you the truth. We have tolerated in our church
some Anabaptists, some Antinomians, and some Seekers, and do so
still at this day, though Seekers of all others have least reason to desire
toleration in [Massachusetts] church fellowship. For they that deny

all churches and church ordinances since the apostacy of Antichrist, they cannot continue in church fellowship but against their own judgment and conscience; and, therefore, four or five of them who openly renounced the church fellowship which they had long enjoyed, the church said amen to their act, and (after serious debate with them, till they had nothing to answer) they were removed from their fellowship. Others carry their dissent more privately and inoffensively, and so are borne withal in much meekness. We are far from arrogating infallibility of judgment to ourselves, or effecting uniformity; uniformity God never required, infallibility he never granted us. We content ourselves with unity in the foundation of religion and of church order. Superstructures we suffer to vary. We have here Presbyterian churches as well as Congregational, and have learned (through grace) to keep the unity of the spirit in the bond of peace. Only, we are loath to be blown up and down (like chaff) by every wind or new notion. . . .

source 33

A Passionate Testimony

Roger Williams

Having done with our transitory, earthly affairs . . . which in comparison of heavenly and eternal [matters] you will say are but as dung and dross, etc., let me now be humbly bold to remember that humanity and piety which I and others have formerly observed in you, and in that hopeful remembrance to crave your gentle audience with patience and mildness . . . .

Be pleased then (honored sir) to remember that thing which we call conscience is of such a nature (especially in Englishmen) as once a Pope of Rome, at the suffering of an Englishman in Rome, himself observed that although it be groundless, false, and deluded, yet it is not by any arguments or torments easily removed. I speak not of the stream of the multitude of all nations, which have their ebbings and flowings in religion (as the longest sword and strongest arm of flesh carries it); but I speak of conscience, a persuasion fixed in the mind and heart of a man, which enforces him to judge . . . and to do so and so with respect to God, His worship, etc.

This conscience is found in all mankind, more or less, in Jews, Turks, Papists, Protestants, pagans, etc. And to this purpose let me freely, without offense, remember you (as I did Mr. Clarke, newly come up from his sufferings among you), I say, remember you of the same story I did him. It was that of William Hartley, in Queen Elizabeth her days, who receiving the sentence of hanging, drawing, etc., spoke confidently (as afterwards he suffered): "What tell you me of hanging, etc? If I had ten thousand millions of lives, I would spend them all for the faith of Rome. . . ."

Roger Williams, Letter to John Endecott, Providence, August, 1651, in *The Bloody Tenent yet More Bloody* (1652), pp. 502-503, 508-509, 513-18.

The Maker and Searcher of our hearts knows with what bitterness I write, as with bitterness of soul I have heard such language as this to proceed from yourself and others, who formerly have fled from (with crying out against) persecutors! You will say, this is your conscience; you will say, you are persecuted, and you are persecuted for your conscience. "No, you are conventiclers, heretics, blasphemers, seducers. You deserve to be hanged; rather than one shall be wanting to hang him, I will hang him myself. I am resolved not to leave an heretic in the country. I had rather so many whores and whoremongers and thieves come among us." Oh sir, you cannot forget what language and dialect this is, whether not the same unsavory and ungodly, blasphemous and bloody, . . . used to all that bowed not to the state golden image of what conscience soever they were. . . .

Oh remember, it is a dangerous combat for the potsherds of the earth to fight with their dreadful potter! It is a dismal battle for poor naked feet to kick against the pricks; it is a dreadful voice from the King of kings and Lord of lords: "Endecott, Endecott, why hunt you me? why imprison you me? why fine, why so bloodily whip? why would you . . . hang and burn me?" Yea, sir, I beseech you [to] remember that it is a dangerous thing to put this to the maybe, to the venture or hazard, to the possibility [that you punish godly men]. "Is it possible," may you well say, "that since I hunt, I hunt not the life of my Saviour and the blood of the Lambe of God? I have fought against many several sorts of consciences; is it beyond all possibility and hazard that I have not fought against God, that I have not persecuted Jesus in some of them?"

Sir, I must be humbly bold to say, that it is impossible for any man or men to maintain their Christ by their sword and to worship a true Christ! To fight against all consciences opposite to theirs, and not to fight against God in some of them and to hunt after the precious life of the true Lord, Jesus Christ? . . . It is but worldly policy and compliance with men and times (God's mercy overruling) that holds your hands from murdering of thousands and ten thousands were your power and command as great as once the bloody Roman Emperor's was.

The truth is (and yourself and others have said it) by your principles such whom you count heretics, blasphemers, seducers, [are necessarily] to be put to death. You cannot be faithful to your principles and consciences if you satisfy them with but imprisonment, fining, whipping, and banishing the heretics, and by saying that banishing is a kind of death, as some chief with you (in my case formerly) have said it. . . .

Oh remember the black catalogue it has pleased the most jealous and righteous God to make of His fiery judgments and most dreadful strokes on eminent and remarkable persecutors, even in this life. . . .

Sir, I know I have much presumed upon your many weighty affairs and thoughts; I end with an humble cry to the Father of Mercies that you may . . . silently commune with your own heart upon your bed. . . . That no sleep may seize upon your eyes, nor slumber upon your eyelids, until your serious thoughts have seriously, calmly, and unchangeably (through help from Christ Jesus) fixed:

First, on a moderation toward the spirits and consciences of all mankind merely differing from or opposing yours with only religious and spiritual opposition.

Secondly, a deep and cordial resolution (in these wonderful, searching, disputing, and dissenting times) to search, to listen, to pray, to fast, and more fearfully, more tremblingly to inquire what the holy pleasure and the holy mysteries of the Most Holy are. . . .

Suggested Readings

The vast literature on Roger Williams is characterized by as much controversy as Williams' own career. A readable and moderate summary of Williams' life is Ola E. Winslow, *Master Roger Williams* (New York: The Macmillan Co., 1957). A representative sampling of opinion may be obtained from Samuel H. Brockunier, *The Irrepressible Democrat: Roger Williams* (New York: The Ronald Press Co., 1940); Henry M. Dexter, *As to Roger Williams* (Boston: Congregational Publishing Co., 1876); Perry Miller, *Roger Williams: His Contribution to the American Tradition* (New York: Bobbs-Merrill Co., Inc., 1953); Alan Simpson, "How Democratic Was Roger Williams?" *William and Mary Quarterly*, 13: 53-67 (January, 1956); and striking but sometimes erroneous accounts of Williams and Cotton in Vernon L. Parrington, *Main Currents in American Thought: The Colonial Mind, 1620-1800* (New York: Harcourt, Brace & World, Inc., 1927). The historiography of Williams is discussed in LeRoy Moore, Jr., "Roger Williams and the Historians," *Church History*, 32: 432-451 (December, 1963).

The best account of John Cotton is Lazar Ziff, *The Career of John Cotton: Puritanism and the American Experience* (Princeton: Princeton University Press, 1962). A recent work which introduces the writings of Cotton is Everett Emerson, *John Cotton* (New York: Twayne Publishers, 1965). A searching estimate of Cotton is presented in Emery Battis, *Saints and Sectaries: Anne Hutchinson and the Antinomian Controversy in the Massachusetts Bay Colony* (Chapel Hill, N.C.: University of North Carolina Press, 1962).

General works dealing with Puritanism in England and America are invaluable for the subjects dealt with in this book. The best starting points are the masterful contributions of Perry Miller, including *Orthodoxy in Massachusetts, 1630-1650* (Cambridge, Mass.: Harvard University Press, 1933); and selected essays in *Errand in the Wilderness* (Cambridge, Mass.: Belknap Press of Harvard University Press, 1956). Of special interest also are Edmund S. Morgan, *The Puritan Dilemma: The Story of John Winthrop* (Boston: Little, Brown & Co., 1958); *Visible Saints: The History of a Puritan Idea* (New York: New York University Press, 1963). A provocative book that challenges Miller's approach to the development of Massachusetts is Darrett B. Rutman, *Winthrop's Boston: Portrait of a Puritan Town, 1630-1649* (Chapel Hill, N.C.: University of North Carolina Press, 1965). Alden T. Vaughn, *New England Frontier: Puritans and Indians 1620-1675* (Boston: Little, Brown & Co., 1965), provides an authoritative examination of Williams and the controversy over the Indian lands. Valuable conflicting studies also include James T. Adams, *The Founding of New England* (Boston: Atlantic Monthly Press, 1921); Samuel E. Morison, *Builders of the Bay Colony* (Boston: Houghton Mifflin Co., 1930); Thomas J. Wertenbaker, *The Puritan Oligarchy* (New York: Charles Scribner's Sons, 1947); Raymond P. Stearns, *The Strenuous Puritan: Hugh Peter, 1598-1660* (Urbana, Ill.: University of Illinois Press, 1954); George L. Haskins, *Law and Authority in Early Massachusetts: A Study in Tradition and Design* (New York: The Macmillan Co., 1960); and Lawrence S. Mayo, *John Endecott* (Cambridge, Mass.: Harvard University Press, 1936).

Among the books concerned with the situation in England one may consult Alan Simpson, *Puritanism in Old and New England* (Chicago: University of Chicago Press, 1956); W. K. Jordan, *The Development of Religious Toleration in England*, 4 vols. (Cambridge, Mass.: Harvard University Press, 1933-1940); Charles H. and Katherine George, *The Puritan Mind of the Protestant Reformation* (Princeton: Princeton University Press, 1961); Champlin Burrage, *Early English Dissenters*, 2 vols. (Cambridge: Cambridge University Press, 1912); Marshall Knappen, *Tudor Puritanism* (Chicago: Chicago University Press, 1938); and the excellent study of William Haller, *Liberty and Reformation in the Puritan Revolution* (New York: Columbia University Press, 1955).